I've Had Enough!

*My Safe Space from the
Liberal Ideology and Narrative*

I've Had Enough!

*My Safe Space from the
Liberal Ideology and Narrative*

Robert J. Ross

JBeam Press
2020

Other Books By Robert J. Ross

Wilbert Thomas Tuttle

Up 'Till Now

Founders' Intent

.

First Printing: 2020

ISBN: 978-1-7339559-5-9

JBeam Press

wwwJBeamPress@comcast.net

Special discounts are available on quantity purchases by corporations, associations, educators, and others. For details, contact the publisher at the above listed address.

U.S. trade bookstores and wholesalers: Please contact JBeam Press at the internet address above

Dedication

To those who routinly practice the Golden Rule.

Contents

Acknowledgements

Thomas Sowell, American economist, social theorist, and senior fellow at Stanford University's Hoover Institute. Mr. Sowell's illuminating insights as presented in his many books and online interviews have provided me with particularly useful perspectives for evaluating current issues.

Professor David Eltis, PhD for his generous assistance confirming estimates from the <u>Slave Data Base</u>. He patiently guided me through the project's complexities to ensure correct usage in this work.

Dave Coverly, award-winning cartoonist whose one panel cartoons have appeared in The Herald-Tribune, Esquire, The Saturday Evening Post, The New York Times, and USA Today. Dave very generously made a particularly appropriate cartoon available for this publication.

Evan Sayet drew on and graciously shared his perspective as a reformed liberal-turned-conservative author and comedian. I sincerely appreciate his willingness to share aspects of his presentation of liberal thoughts and rationales.

Kathleen Brush, PhD MBA, management consultant and author has been extremely generous in her time reviewing critical portions of this book and offered particularly useful insights and comment. Thank you so much, Kathleen.

I also owe special thanks to ordained minister and founder and chairman of the Racial Policy Center Mychal Massie for his views on racial issues and willingness to share them in my work.

As with every aspect of my life, I sincerely thank my patient, supportive, and loving wife Joye, who gets me through the challenges and makes all times so much more worth living.

Foreword

Preface

Having experienced the peerless success of our Constitutionally-based government and open markets, it seems surreal that anyone would seriously challenge them with structures run by an elite few and a history of misery. That's precisely what's happening, though.

The far-left promotes the same system that gave rise to the oppressions, hostility towards its population and inefficiency as we witness in Venezuela. Right before our eyes, that once-vibrant country with the largest oil reserves in the world, saw its annual GDP plunge from 5.3% to -18.6% and its 2015 poverty rate reach an astounding 33.1%[1]. Ruling elites there suspended constitutional rights and substituted the entire Supreme Court. Violent crime has risen dramatically - 10x ours in 2016. Remarkably, very large numbers of American voters support like-minded leftists here.

The more extreme left-wing movement began as activists stretched traditional Democrat Party platform planks, then intensified them under such banners as Social and Economic Justice, Black Lives Matter, Know Their Names, and Me Too. Despite these noble-sounding causes, we've regularly watched their most senior leaders preside over vast programs to reduce poverty while the rate has stabilized or increased since 1986[2]. We've literally watched neighborhoods burn and violent attacks on police rise; liberal elites have been complicit in broad, complex, illegal schemes such as a Russian collusion hoax abetted by a fabricated intelligence dossier.

In public, far leftist operatives have become increasingly violent by staging riots, looting, desecration and destruction of public and private property, and bodily assaults. Worse yet, sympathetic city council members, mayors, and governors lightly brush off, accept, or even abet the criminal aspects of many otherwise legitimate demonstrations. The mainstream media - broadcast, social, and print - are reliable and willing partners in support of these ideologues by heavily weighting prevailing narratives. Today the broader movement could be accurately described as the Socialist Supremacy.

When confronted with the counter-culture and violence on TV every night, it's easy to become despondent or agitated, extremely uncomfortable, or even fearful. Is there another option? Should you demand and seek a physical "safe space" that so many college presidents and administrators create where emotionally and intellectually-fragile students can bury their heads and avoid debating ideas?

Not at all! Thoughtful, informed citizens have no need for a designated location that bans challenging ideas and ideologies, or to fabricate pretexts like "hate speech" to justify inadequate moral and legal justifications for trampling the First Amendment's guarantee of free speech.

What to do? Review headlines, read some of the accompanying stories, and examine a few topics in depth to compare with actual life experience. Read original sources, such as Department of Justice reports, Census Bureau, and FBI crime information, which is quite easily done on the internet. Compare media stories with the permanence and universality of human behaviors, beliefs, and values that have stood the test of millennia.

Absent an actual physical threat, "safe spaces" aren't defined geographically on campus or anywhere else. An enduring safe space is intellectual – knowing what you believe, stand for, and why. People with that knowledge are equally comfortable in an integrated dormitory, listening to a public speaker presenting differing opinions, or peacefully protesting.

This is not a research paper or doctoral thesis, but an examination of current pivotal events and narratives. It considers a number of decades of life experience with my wife of 46 years, two children, five grandchildren, 12 moves in 28 years of military assignments in the United States, the Republic of Panama, and the Republic of Korea, and operational deployments to the Mideast, Bolivia, Honduras, Thailand, and Japan. Throw in three brothers for good measure.

I've Had Enough! presents the ideas, facts, and logic that comprise my safe space from the far-left's ideology and its supporting narrative. Readers may agree with them or not. For those who don't, this is a useful basis for identifying differences and initiating a dialogue.

Introduction

T he intense emotions, motivations, and actions shaping our political and economic future emanate from the eternal brawl for vast amounts of power and spoils flowing through the structures of government and the economy.

Today's radical left is attacking not only the existing Constitutionally-defined political structure, but the open market system as well. Free markets reward individual efforts and embrace equal opportunity and individual choices. Socialism promises (but has never delivered) equal outcomes and it answers only to an omnipotent centralized government elite. The inherent differences are mutually exclusive and inevitably invite conflict.

A knowledge of world and American history goes a long way towards creating a balanced perspective of conflict events that disciples promote as calamitous: rampant national racism, unchecked police violence against black Americans, and mankind's doomsday role in climate change. Watching events unfold in high definition on a 65" color television can be frightening, especially when the broadcaster's primary purpose is political advocacy and profitability instead of reporting facts within their historical context and airing a contrasting perspective.

None of those and other causes deserve blind allegiance, but all of them certainly merit open evaluation against relevant empirical data. Such debates used to be a keystone of the college experience – to hear and critically evaluate opposing perspectives. Not so much anymore. Delicate students who cannot support bumper sticker slogans or opposition to another candidate through effective thinking, historical perspective, or current facts simply shout them down. And too many of their instructors and administrators stand right beside them.

People who are oblivious to these events are indirect supporters of their worst outcomes, being too detached to knowledgeably cast ballots for candidates with better solutions rather than hucksters selling an easily-digested, emotionally-comforting, dodges. In Baltimore, MD, a city that has one of the highest urban murder rates in the country, a majority of its voters continue to elect candidates with the same old promises to cure the conditions without ever doing so.

It's especially troubling to see young crusaders categorically condemn and all too often literally tear apart institutions, a targeted race, or the country when some past, present, or perceived reality conflicts with their ideas. They, who have yet to contribute any enduring value to society, are completely mindless of their forebears' herculean efforts to develop language, governments, laws, national systems of electrification, transportation, communications, space travel, defense, commerce and finance, arts, food production, water distribution, sanitation, and the world's best medical capabilities. And all were accomplished through a revolutionary war, a civil war, two world wars, another in Korea, ones in the jungle and desert, as well as an ongoing lethal Middle Eastern conflict nearing its 20th anniversary.

Today's ultra-liberal violent protestors, anarchists, and thugs are completely oblivious to those broad past accomplishments. They have no knowledge of "... every painful step and every world-shaking contest by which mankind has worked and fought its way from savage isolation to organic social life."[3] They have no workable ideas or résumés for improving society, but ravage Portland, OR, Seattle, WA, Chicago, IL, Minneapolis, MN, Atlanta, GA, and other cities.

I've had enough.

I've Had Enough!

Chapter 1: Imagine

"It isn't so much that liberals are ignorant.
It's just that they know so many things that aren't so."

President Ronald Reagan

G enerations of Americans are baffled by frequent, violent, and lengthy riots in their cities, the kind they only associated with impoverished 3rd-world countries. Even more bewildering, though, are the perpetrators who've grown up in the most accepting, affluent, and secure country in history. "Why are they doing it? How do you understand or make any sense of it? Can you?"

In our brief history, free markets have contributed immeasurably to rapid growth and unmatched national prosperity. When combined with our pluralistic government and security from lethal military threats, that may be too much of a good thing. Many Americans up through their mid-40s have no recollection of the USSR's worldwide conquests and threatened nuclear attacks, being drafted for compulsory military service, manifest discrimination, and 16% home mortgage rates. Having such memories behind us isn't all bad, of course, but it does set a stage for renewed directions that *are* bad. With those "biggest and baddest" dragons slain by preceding generations, how can today's ideological knights prove their worth, righteousness, and moral purity to themselves and peers?

This is the era of activists who declare an awakening from the slumber of social apathy towards what they believe is unprecedented discrimination, injustice, and persecution. They draw from backgrounds and employ thought processes to arrive at a completely contradictory view of past and present America. But how? How did they develop such a divergent outlook and where do they imagine it's taking them… and everyone else?

Increasingly, many of them find or invent new dragons that are far less consequential than those of yore. Too many of today's activists grew up (or perhaps simply aged-up) with helicopter parents constantly hovering over them, shielding them from key lessons about people, tolerance, physical and mental challenges, and opposing ideas. Parents absolved them of responsibilities, sacrifice, and the reality of working to earn for needs and wants: food, housing, clothes, heating, and plumbing were always "just there", naturally-occurring conditions like clouds and trees.

Earlier generations often learned universal lessons about human nature, tolerance, and morality through faith, but polls show the role of faith is diminishing in Americans' lives.[4] What's taken its place, or have those lessons simply been lost?

The synthetic lifestyle continued through 12 years of government schools where competitive playground activities were banished decades ago. Extracurricular sports adopted a pandering "everyone's a winner at everything" mentality with trophies awarded all around. With very little absolute authority, expectations and boundaries became blurred.

Many went on to college, where policies and professors perpetuated and reinforced nascent ideas about life, work, threats, responsibility, morals, and rights. Here, they were also subjected to an intensified drumbeat of socialist teachings, perspectives, and dogma without learning their fatal consequences or balancing those lessons with alternative socio-economic structures, ideologies, and historical realities. Millions can turn down food if it isn't vegan, whole, or organic, and now wear the uniform only if they choose to.

From provisioned, secure, and screened lives, they reasonably believe these conditions are universal, and are astonished to discover otherwise. Some venture from segregated graduations searching for soul-fulfilling employment. With untried, unseasoned knowledge and increasingly-fervent social passions, they seek employers who will pay what they require for their needs, wants, and crushing student debt (they certainly never considered military service for GI Bill education benefits). It becomes considerably more difficult when their expensive knowledge is of dubious relevance to what society will pay for, a reality they add to a growing list of socio-economic injustice inflicted upon them and others.

Life's disparities become their dragons, and they have time, energy, and a fundamental need for relevance to crusade against them. These knights join ranks not to preserve or build upon structures that secured and nurtured their lives, but to confront them in Quixotic hopes of changing the elemental nature of humanity.

They conclude that America only achieved its primacy in the world through a hidden, wicked past and it now wallows in extensive injustice, from wealth and income to housing, education, and community safety. They feel enlightened to a consciousness of newly-revealed horrors that define America's rotten core - that discrimination is embedded to one degree or another in every policy, institution, and practice. It all needs to be fixed and they are responsible for doing so. Everyone else is racist or deplorable.

As Douglas Murray reminds us in *The Madness of Crowds: Gender, Race, and Identity*, "… a demonstration of virtue demands an overstating of the problem, which then causes an amplification of the problem." That "go big or go home" challenge demands an equally amplified solution, one that many of the faithful foot soldiers and supporting power brokers implement with violent calls to replace opposing ideas with a single dogma and a bountiful open-market economy with socialism.

Without realizing that great doesn't mean perfect and flawed doesn't mean failed, they've awakened. They are Woke.

The far-left and woke aren't Liberals or Democrats in the John F. Kennedy mold. They and today's much more radical Democrat leaders openly, even hotly, promote a socialist structure in line with past or current regimes in China, Cuba, Venezuela, and 1940s Germany. They are fully awakened and bolstered in their beliefs through actual and virtual social groups, kindred news sources, and fellow event participants. Increasingly confident and assured of the righteousness of their cause, they nobly march on to liberate the oppressed, the discriminated, and the forgotten.

Wokes understand that people learn behaviors through family, faith, school, friends, and admired leaders. Too much of what people learn, they reason, leads to judgments that result in differences, discrimination, and injustice. Therefore, the ideology goes, eliminate the sources of behaviors and judgments and you rid society of injustice.

That simplified analysis makes campaigns against the nuclear family, faith, personal property, and nations a logical imperitive. John Lennon expressed similar ideas in his song *Imagine,* which he stated was "...virtually the Communist Manifesto". While entertaining and inspiring to some, the mirthful lyrics have no intersection with reality. Next, fill school curricula with revisionist history classes, denigrate free market capitalism, and make any past atrocity the main lesson about national character. Omit similar or worse exploits by the rest of the world. Abandon critical thinking and conclude that truth doesn't exist - there're as many "truths" as there are people's opinions.

Some of the rank and file pursue the cause to the extreme, joining the violent ranks within Black Lives Matter and ANTIFA. Those factions of Woke supremacists, like all other supremacists, practice every means possible to achieve their end: disrupting visiting speakers, assailing public figures in restaurants, censorship, intimidation, looting, fire-bombing and ransacking police precincts, other government offices, and businesses, physical assaults that are sometimes fatal – they deem it all necessary in the campaign for tolerance, fairness, and justice.

While they and particularly-radical political proponents like U.S. Senator Bernie Sanders (D-VT), U.S. Representative Alexandria Ocasio-Cortez (D-NY), and acquiescent party leaders march towards socialism, none of them discuss how they'll deal with the half of Americans who oppose the tyrannical idea. Past socialists found several very effective solutions to the problem of non-compliance: expulsion, "re-education", gulags, bullets, and gas chambers.

What's missing from this progression of development and conclusions? First, a perilous ignorance of humans' primal nature and how it's revealed itself since people started walking upright. Second is experience, particularly in a demanding job, being responsible for others, travelling overseas or living in a socialist country to compare their freedoms and quality of life with that here. Finally, knowing what no professor, history book, friend, parent, or chat room explained: that the U.S. is the foremost guardian against international tyranny and that it's the most affluent and tolerant. It's been and remains a beacon and destination for immigrants the world over.

Differences over structure and ideology have to be resolved with proposals and votes instead of pyrotechnics and violence. The nation rightfully prides itself on deciding such sweeping matters in accordance with the rule of law, the topic of the next chapter.

I've Had Enough!

Chapter 2: Rules

Rule 16. The challenged has the right to choose his own weapon, unless the challenger gives his honor he is no swordsman; after which, however, he cannot decline any second species of weapon proposed by the challenged.

Irish Code of Honor [regarding duels], 1777[5]

Whenever two or more people get together, there's a need for rules to guide their conduct and peacefully settle disputes; and that need rises dramatically with larger and more diverse populations. Rules that withstand the test of time across multiple civilizations consider, rather than oppose, the laws of nature - those primal human behaviors embedded in our DNA. They also embrace selected principles that are absolute, rather than relative to the age, principles such as communism is evil, the reality of binary genders, and that humans act in their own self-interest.

The most fundamental self-interest is survival. If you want to get a hint of where we'll go when threatened, look at grocers' shelves during the onset of a hurricane or the China virus. And that's just canned soup, hand sanitizer, and toilet paper!

While all creatures have the instinct to physically survive enemies and perilous conditions, humans exhibit an additional dimension of this powerful instinct: emotional survival. A common manifestation of this potent drive is the need for relevancy rather than seeing yourself as a faceless, inconsequential nobody. Some people achieve psychological/emotional relevance through study, honing artistic talents, leadership, or seeking excellence in physical pursuits. Nurturing is supremely relevant to many.

Other people, however, find themselves devoid of talents they can hone to any degree of notability, or they choose not to expend the usually considerable effort to do so. They develop an increasing sense of insignificance over time, an inward recognition of defeat – which fails to meet their innate need for emotional survival. And no one aspires to be a failure.

Rules are commonly codified and enforced by central figures that world history knows as pharaohs, emperors, kings and queens, emirs, chiefs, premieres, dictators, prime ministers, and presidents. Most of them acquired and maintained their authority through brute force, as they have recently in China, Russia, Cuba, and Venezuela.

The source of *our* governments' authority, however, is provided by the governed themselves when they cede a portion of the individual rights endowed by their creator to the collective government. Abraham Lincoln reaffirmed the principle, "What I do say is, that no man is good enough to govern another man, without that other's consent. I say this is the leading principle - the sheet anchor of American republicanism." Although familiar to us, this was an unprecedented concept when the Founding Fathers introduced their moral ideals over two centuries ago. That bold experiment has endured here and proliferated elsewhere ever since.

A corollary to the concept of the governed ceding a portion of their individual rights to government is that they cannot convey rights they do not have. If you, for example, don't have the individual right to force another to provide you with health care, you cannot cede what you don't have to government, and it cannot Constitutionally exercise that authority.

We Americans have developed an extensive set of rules for our increasingly complex society. While there are ponderous volumes (or megabytes nowadays) of municipal ordinances and state and federal laws, they're all predicated on core moral ideals embodied in our federal Constitution.

The Founders understood that we humans always act in our own self-interest. This is even true with someone as benevolent as Saint Mother Teresa (fortunately for the impoverished of Calcutta, her self-interest of sacrificing everything to help the poor coincided with the needs of those she cared for). James Madison's observation "If men were angels, no government would be necessary" recognized that too many politicians' self-interests are *not* aligned with the governed. In response, the Founding Fathers' Constitution deliberately structured a government with divided powers.

With a government now authorized and established comes the matter of purpose – to what end do we create a government with authority to forcefully exercise its authority? In the United States, the response is simple: to secure our individual rights. That leads directly to the matter of positive and negative rights. Negative rights are those that others cannot violate, and you can enjoy them without the labor of others – they simply have to respect them. For example, you have the right to liberty, which people are not allowed to violate by kidnapping you.

In direct contrast are positive rights – the enjoyment of goods and services that can only be realized through the labor of others, such as health care. Government-protected negative rights do not include guarantees of material goods like food, shelter, and clothing, nor of services - everything from mowing your yard to health care. If they were, government would often have to compel providers to accept less compensation than they would willingly accept, the difference being forced servitude. Liberals love the idea of positive rights.

Two other notes on government-enforced rights: we *do* have the right to hate people and to utter speech that others find insensitive and offensive. Everyone else, of course, has the right to ignore us, socially isolate us, and boycott our products and services. While we have clear protections against *physical* assault, we have no such legal protections against others' offending speech, gestures, music, signs, or ideas. If you're offended, counter the ideas with better ones or simply walk away.

In addition to securing our rights, societies also have to grapple with the very thorny issue of allocating products and services among its members, which in a modern society like ours ranges from the very basics of food, shelter, clothing, and health care to electricity, internet access, education, and entertainment.

Should society distribute resources equally to everyone, that is, to enforce equal outcomes? Today's progressives emphatically respond with a resounding "Yes, of course!"

Other liberals prefer 19th century German socialist revolutionary Karl Marx's formula, "From each according to their ability, and to each according to their needs"? This option immediately raises questions about who decides what those needs are for hundreds of millions of different people in an even greater number of different circumstances, and how much of a worker's earnings the state can take to give to them. How do you prevent unbridled abuses? You cannot, a truth that liberals ignore in their Utopian crusades.

Another allocation method, which historically results in the greatest overall prosperity is open markets, where everyone evaluates the costs and values of products and services and votes accordingly with their dollars. Too many Americans, however, truly believe that someone *else* is responsible for providing their personal needs and solving their problems. They are convinced that some government bureaucrat, rather than themselves, family, faith, charities, and business, is that "someone else." After all, that's what liberal candidates, politicians, and public figures keep telling them.

Officials who make or strongly influence government decisions to collect and disburse tax revenues, ban or limit fundamental activities, and who allocate favors wield immeasurable power – an aphrodisiac and significantly fulfilling form of relevance in itself. Such an allure to riches that flow too easily from government-held offices regularly attracts a personality type that demands undisputed authority, a fawning public, and revels in the ability to punish enemies.

Unfortunately, they comprise too large a share of officials who privately harbor contempt for true public service and treat their government position as a throne with an almost incontestable license to do their bidding or that of their handlers and supporters.

Living successfully in our Constitutional republic isn't a spectator affair, but one that demands members who know how it works and actively engaged in its conduct. There's no on-call version of Ghostbusters to remedy bad government. Neither the courts, politicians, nor the Constitution give you freedom, you have to build it yourself.

If this is beginning to sound a bit involved, it is. With the world's third largest population, a broad variety of races, ethnicities, faiths, and regional differences, and jobs and careers that provide vastly different rewards in an open marketplace, it can be overwhelming. That's especially true for those who are uneducated, disinterested, or simply choose not to put forth the necessary effort to achieve their goals.

In 2020, irresponsible mobs across the country became frustrated to the point of violently lashing out over aggravated incidents in order to advance anarchist agendas or vent any number of individual frustrations and grievances. On June 8, a rabble in Seattle, WA declared six city blocks around a police precinct as the "Capitol Hill Autonomous Zone", or CHAZ. They erected barricades and denied entry to the police and firefighters. Democrat Mayor Jenny Durkan famously described the zone as "four blocks in Seattle that is more like a block party atmosphere. It's not an armed takeover. It's not a military junta. We will make sure that we will restore this but we have block parties and the like in this part of Seattle all the time ... there is no threat right now to the public."

As those mayor, city council, occupiers, and many sympathetic Seattle residents soon discovered, governance within the CHAZ became considerably more complicated than simply declaring it autonomous, barring the police, and allowing occupants "to work things out". In the absence of societal rules and a trained means to enforce them, chaos was brewing.

Following two deaths and four wounded there, Mayor Durkan reversed course and police cleared the area on July 1, 2020. Seattle Police Chief Carmen Best submitted a letter to the liberal City Council informing them of the consequences of their recently-legislated ban on police use of non-lethal crowd dispersal tools like tear gas and pepper spray. Chillingly, it said "The Council legislation gives officers no ability to safely intercede to preserve property in the midst of a large, violent crowd."[6] The council took no action and Chief Best resigned.

The council's message? That you're on your own if a riotous mob's going to burn your home or business and assault or murder your family. City Council member Lisa Herbold ,who also serves as Vice Chair of the Finance and Housing Committee, went even farther in October when she floated legislation through the budget process to exempt from prosecution all misdemeanor crimes by anyone suffering from poverty, homelessness, addiction, or mental illness. These crimes account for about 90% of all citywide misdemeanor cases. Seattle's former public safety advisor commented, "This would absolutely open the floodgates for crime in Seattle, even worse than what we often currently struggle with. It's basically a blank check for anybody committing theft, assault, harassment (and) trespass to continue without disruption from our criminal justice system."[7] As of Dec 1, 2020, the city recorded 47 homicides compared to 28 the year before.[8]

Down the coast in San Francisco, turning a blind eye to shoplifting is costing businesses so much that Walgreens drug stores is closing its eighth store. Next, of course, the mayor and city council will scream "racist" because minorities are underserved.

The elected leadership of Minneapolis told its citizens to comply with criminals' requests: give them your wallet, purse and money as a way to reduce the violence. If you're at knifepoint, that's useful advice, but city leaders are charged with maintaining a level of law, order, and public safety to prevent the robbery in the first place.

They never learn the fundamentals while wallowing in microaggression theory; Liberalism at its most destructive.

Chapter 3: What Liberals Want

Liberalism is totalitarianism with a human face.

Thomas Sowell, Economist and Social Theorist

L et me first clarify who I'm referring to as a "liberal". In the 1960s Republicans were reputed to advocate smaller government, individual responsibility, more individual liberty, and a smaller budget – with a sizeable amount of it appropriated for national defense. After all, the federal government's foremost responsibility is to defend the nation and we were hip deep in the Cold War with the USSR. Democrats advocated smaller defense budgets, more government-run programs to manage people's lives, and ever more taxes to pay for them.

The landscape has evolved since then. Now, administrations of both parties spend way beyond annual revenues. Republicans generally remain more committed to military readiness; Democrats continue to foster ever bigger government solutions to every legacy individual social issue, as well as newly implemented ones.

Democrats have also changed their name - not formally, but in politico-speak to appeal to new, younger, and increasingly more radical audiences who are under-informed about human nature, government, and history. Democrats referred to themselves as Liberals, which aptly describes their policies and is also good for marketing to youth and/or free spirits who revolt at the idea of being bound to anything "conservative".

For over a decade now we've heard the re-branding title "Progressive" enter the lexicon of the left. Some just consider it a refresh of the time-worn titles "Democrat" and "Liberal", while others see it as a clear new direction: using the power of government to *force* businesses to operate by their rules.[9] Increasingly, we also hear liberals describe themselves as Woke, or having an awakened or better awareness of social, racial, and economic matters. The term "liberals" is used in this book with an emphasis on far-left Liberals, Progressives, and the self-described Woke.

What do political leaders of both parties want? Realistically, their objective is to "get our guys in charge of local, state, and federal governments so we can impose our socio-economic-political structure on everyone else, enrich ourselves, bask in prestige, punish opponents, and disburse appointments and money to stay in power."

The crux of the debate, then, is knowing what changes far-leftists want to make to the historically very successful republic and free market. Their publicly-stated goal is to rid society of greed and injustice and to achieve equal outcomes for all. Actions, however, reveal significantly different intents; here's a Cliff Notes version of current liberal positions:

Acceptable to Liberals:[10]
More central control by a larger federal government
Higher taxes to pay for more government and its programs
Abolish Immigration and Customs Enforcement

Less individual liberty	Abolish the electoral college
Downsize the military	Defunding police, no guns
Eliminate all fossil fuels	Green New Deal
Promote secularism	Pack the courts with liberals
Promote late-term abortions	Sell baby parts
Abolish private health care	Mandate health insurance
Open all US borders	Maintain an underclass
Rioting	Looting
Attacking police	Intimidation, censorship
Burning businesses	Anarchy

Unacceptable to Liberals:

Individual responsibility	Mrs. Butterworth's Syrup
Critical thinking	*Gone With the Wind*
Open markets	Elmer Fudd cartoons
Open debate	Paw Patrol cartoons
Mary Poppins	Aunt Jemima pancake mix
Eskimo Pie ice cream bars	Uncle Ben's Rice

Aside from everyone who doesn't agree with them, woke liberals believe there are no bad or evil people, just some who are misunderstood or the product of bad environments. All those problems, they contend, can be resolved with new government programs that provide these misdirected souls with compassionate attention instead of leaving their development and fate to the uncontrolled vagaries of family, faith groups, charities, and service organizations. The programs, of course, will come at the expense of family budgets and liberty.

It's very useful to recognize how uniquely different governments are from the hundreds of thousands of other organizations throughout our communities, states, and country. Governments stand absolutely apart from every other organization in one essential way: they have legal, coercive enforcement authority and power to deprive citizens of their Constitutional rights to life, liberty, and the pursuit of happiness through execution, incarceration, and monetary fines and property seizures. Consequently, governments (or more precisely, those who hold the reins of government authority and power) bear very close and constant scrutiny.

Liberals appeal to voters through a carefully-orchestrated playbook embellished with the best presentations that Hollywood and media can produce. They know the public doesn't want to deal with adult realities, but would rather listen to soothing, starry-eyed bedtime stories of free college, food, and health car; government-guaranteed jobs and housing. No responsibilities – just soak the rich to pay for everyone else. Unfortunately, too many uninformed voters eagerly accept it at face value.

Many liberal positions, plans, and rationales have the tone of a late-night college freshman BS session, and "A lie repeated often enough becomes accepted truth" goes an axiom variously attributed to propaganda experts Joseph Goebbels, Vladimir Lenin, Adolph Hitler, and others.

Fundamentals of Modern Liberals / Progressives / Wokes

1. **America is evil**. "Our nation was founded in 1619 on the evils of slavery and white Europeans invading peaceful, defenseless native minorities. Much of that evil still exists in the form of boundless systemic and intrinsic racism and social injustice. The country runs on imperialism (Viet Nam war, Grenada, Iraq, Afghanistan), greed, and minority oppression."

I've Had Enough!

Yes, slavery existed in North America in the century and a half before the nation's founding, and other dark events certainly occurred afterwards. Knowing history and the nature of man, though, none of it should be surprising. Slavery certainly wasn't confined to North America; in 1650, more English were enslaved in Africa than Africans enslaved in English colonies.[11] Forcing wartime prisoners into unpaid servitude was common to societies that preceded ours and the practice endures in some countries today.

Fortunately, early Americans recognized every person's natural right to life, liberty, and the pursuit of happiness and have taken considerable steps to enforce that right and continue doing so.

Note: Mauritania is the last nation in the world to formally outlaw slavery, which it did in 2007. However, as much as 20% of the population is still estimated to be enslaved - prompting President Trump to revoke trade benefits with that nation.

Against the historical realities of slavery since our founding through the Civil War, serious observers must also consider the other side of the ledger. Namely, what has the nation contributed to its own population, world order, and mankind's benefit in the subsequent 156 years since 1865?

While there will always be more work to do, slave descendants have fared better in America than their counterparts have in ancestral lands. Mychal Massie, (black) founder and chairman of the Racial Policy Center asks, "What are the chances the Obama woman would have been more than a maid or laundry worker had her ancestors stayed in Africa? Even if she were able to slither her way into an African capital as a despot's wife, she'd have been skewered for having flaunted usufruct[1] as her personal ATM as she did here."[12]

While condemning the country, critics ignore the annual $32b of official development aid the United States provided to over 100 countries just last year, and the millions of private citizens who made monetary donations to survivors of such disasters as the 2010

---

[1] Use and profits from something belonging to another

18

earthquake in Haiti ($1.5b), the 2004 Indian Ocean tsunami ($1.3b), and unknown fellow citizens after 2005's Hurricane Katrina ($4.3b).

Woke liberals harangue about the evil USA without realizing it's the nation that liberated the whole of east Asia from Japanese domination and the world from Nazi tyranny. After winning wars on foreign soil, liberals don't recall that American "conquerors" voluntarily withdrew from, rather than occupied and pillaged the resources of Cuba, Morocco, Algeria, Germany, France, Italy, Norway, Austria, Japan, the Philippines, the Republics of Korea and Panama, Grenada, Kuwait, Iraq, and Afghanistan. Americans left all those populations to create their own government, practice their own religions, and reap the benefits of their natural resources and cultures.

2. **Government.** "We know full well that this controlling institution exists for four basic reasons. The first is to ensure equal outcomes for everyone, regardless of whether they conduct themselves responsibly or not. After all, we're all people, and everyone needs some income, housing, health care, and a guaranteed retirement plan".

"The second justification for government is to disburse government money", the source of which is never questioned by the less informed (after all, it's "government money", right? It's just there). More knowledgeable liberals feel that the government is simply and quite justifiably *recovering* perverted gains from evil rich people and abusive businesses that amassed their filthy, ill-gotten lucre by victimizing workers. Since they wrongfully obtained their wealth, government has a *moral obligation* to recover and "re-distribute" it to liberal voters and supporters through a plethora of taxes, credits, programs, and projects.

Note: Income that liberals hunger to *re*-distribute was never *distributed* in the first place, it was *earned* by those offering a product or service that others valued enough to pay for.

Upset with Amazon founder Jeff Bezos because he's the richest person in the world for the third year in a row? Then you and fellow liberals are free to boycott Amazon. Ditto for Microsoft.

These proponents have no interest in how to actually *acquire* wealth, just different schemes to disburse what they assume always existed. Has it helped? Despite decades of liberal largesse that promised to improve minorities' quality of life and safety, the murder rate among Blacks in 1960 was one-half of what it became 20 years later after a legacy of liberal policies and programs.

"Government's third basic role is directing large and small matters in your life, then imposing laws that incentivize obedience and punish defiance." Liberal leaders are confident they know best how to educate your children and care for your elderly relatives. They know how many workers of every skill level in every job should be paid and how to structure their retirement programs. Their keen insights into the human condition will create never-ending programs to relieve you of responsibility for your conditions.

"Finally, liberal governments exist to address all wrongs that our elites discover, amplify, and devising solutions to. Our government will save society by exposing "microaggressions" and a panoply of sins committed by America and its white European majority."

Liberals are quite content to divert earnings from your family's needs to the tax man for the monumental amount of required government spending to staff and conduct these fanciful efforts, and do so without empirical proof of their effectiveness. Your role is to sit down and write checks with lots of zeros at the end. Then you can blindly conform in the secure knowledge that your overlords are the self-declared smartest people in the room.

3. **"Socialism** is the best structure for organizing our society and the economy. We'll call our version *Democratic* Socialism to make it fair, opposed to free markets in a republic that are mean and oppressive."

As Dr. Thomas Sowell quips, "Socialism in general has a record of failure so blatant that only an intellectual could ignore or evade it". Still, proponents adamantly advance socialism as a vital component of a promised end state without greed, envy, and discrimination. Realistically, those behaviors are inherent in human nature; we can limit them at best, as the U.S. demonstrates, but not eradicate them from our DNA.

The modifier "Democratic" seemingly softens socialism's repugnant realities. It isn't describing a resulting social order, however, but how the structure's champions come to power – through the existing process of elections. In that regard, the "father of Democratic Socialism" may well be socialist Adolf Hitler, since he too legitimately came to power in the 1933 Weimar Republic.

Socialism's proponents never lead by example, as exemplified by then-congressional candidate (D-NY) Alexandria Ocasio-Cortez wearing a $3,505 outfit to pose for photo-op with city construction workers. This admitted Democratic Socialists of America member and others haven't lived under the system they promote as a workers' paradise whose wretched truths are exposed everywhere it's been tried and currently exists. Unaccountable strongmen invariably morph this socio-economic model from a promised fantasyland to a totalitarian state like the Greater German Reich, North Korea, Cambodia, Russia, and China.

So why are liberals so eager to embrace and install it? Other than a minority of naïve true believers, proponents embrace it for one primary reason: POWER. Power to control others through police-enforced laws, the military, the economy, education, and the media. Socialism centralizes power to a much greater extent than a distributed market economy where *everyone* has a voice in determining products, prices and purchases. Proponents also know they won't bear any personal consequences for bad decisions, a consideration that keeps *individual* market participants much more chaste in their spending.

Those who are unaware of the past aren't prepared to challenge socialists' glowing claims. When someone else does, liberals respond with conceited conviction, "Of course we're aware of past failures, but they didn't know what *we* know, and *we'll* get it right. Narcissism and ignorance are prerequisites to woke progressivism.

Human nature certainly plays a role in the struggle, too. The dimension that progressives understand all too well is people's desire to avoid conflict by trading liberty for safety (in the end, they lose both). A large segment of the population, especially ardent nurturers, unconditionally gravitates like submissive lemmings to assurances they can enjoy lives as seen in so many Hallmark Christmas movies.

Other sides of human nature, though, undermine socialism's doctrine for producing and allocating goods and services. We all want to maximize gain and minimize pain – get more and pay less, to fly first class on a coach ticket (except the airlines, which want to charge you the price of a first-class ticket for a coach seat). People are also most intimately attuned to their own efforts, situations, and sacrifices, and believe they're contributing more than the next guy or gal, so certainly they deserve more than socialists allocate to them. They constantly clamor for more, more, and more that leaders have to provide or face defeat at the next election by someone who's even more liberal.

To provide it, socialist leaders have to borrow, borrow, and borrow until there're no more lenders. Then the house of cards tumbles, and history has predictably repeated itself. Former British Prime Minister Margaret Thatcher concisely summarized socialism's impracticality in a 1976 Thames Television interview, "Socialist governments traditionally do make a financial mess. They always run out of other people's money."

4. **Abolish Open Markets.** "Capitalism can only succeed through the cruel, immoral exploitation of others - especially Blacks and Hispanics. We *must* transition to socialism."

> *"In general, 'the market' is smarter than the smartest of its individual participants,"*
>
> Robert L. Bartley, Wall Street Journal editor

Actually, the open market system is the *most* moral, as it's based on every individual's voluntary choices instead of faceless government bureaucrats directing what to produce in what quantity and quality, and who gets how much at what price. Open markets are also color blind (ours resulted in increased pay for Blacks during Reconstruction). Capitalism isn't without its flaws, which requires the minimum regulation possible to check them, such as the Sherman Anti-trust Act and public utility regulators.

Since Wokes claim this economic system is the most oppressive, we'd expect a greater proportion of oppressed workers in countries with more rich capitalists. The truth is quite the opposite. The U.S. has over 25 times more billionaires than Africa, yet the average of African countries' poverty rates is $3^1/_2$ times the U.S. rate. The U.S. has 1.8x more billionaires than Europe and Scandinavia and a lower poverty rate than the average of those countries' poverty rates as well.[13]

Critics consistently omit the fact that open-market businesses cannot compel people to work for them or to buy their products or services. Those same critics don't challenge themselves to start businesses and implement all the ideas they say no one else will. Nor do liberals recognize the element of risk involved in starting a business: 20% of new ones don't survive past two years, and half fail by the end of their fifth year[14]. They also omit any discussion of who other than workers has a claim to revenues: initial investors, current owners, vendors and suppliers, distributors, utilities and insurers, and local, state, and federal governments.

Most American workers are employed by small businesses and publicly-traded businesses are owned by shareholders that include pension funds and individual retirement accounts (IRAs). Most Americans, therefore, are also significant beneficiaries of profitable businesses.

A recognized flaw in *all* economic system is cronyism, whereby special interests of all parties influence elected officials of all parties to use the force of government to pick winners and losers.

5. **"Globalism** is an equalizer for the world's masses - especially those oppressed by white people. If a more centralized and authoritarian government is good for America, shouldn't the entire world reap the rewards of a single *global* authority?"

Because the Founding Fathers clearly recognized the limitations of a central government ruling even a handful of states, they enumerated those few powers it was authorized to exercise over all of them; all other powers would be vested with those states. Now with 50 states, the task of governance is manifestly more complex. Elevating the task to a global level is impractical and undesirable.

I've Had Enough!

Could such a body make better decisions and enact better policies or state and national governments do for 330m Americans speaking 350 languages and practicing 1,585 religions in a sweeping array of cultures and occupations across deserts, tropics, plains, and mountains, each with different climates?[15] No, it could not.

The United Nations Universal Declaration of Human Rights proclaimed by that body's General Assembly in 1948 is a foundation for the movement to do so, however.[16] Many of its included rights mimic those in our own Constitution. The embodied *positive* rights, however, should be goals that societies' members achieve through a highly-developed sense of morality and robust economies instead of forcefully exacting resources from one group to disperse to others.

The Document's Article 23, for example, declares that all workers are entitled to remuneration "worthy of human dignity". Who decides what amount *that* is? If their work doesn't earn employers enough to pay it, who's responsible for making up the difference and why should they?

Article 25 establishes the right for everyone to have food, clothing, housing, medical care, social services, and "security" in old age or unemployment or sickness. Who determines how much is adequate? Again, for those whose contributions are insufficient to pay for their needs, who does government expropriate from to provide them? How do you prevent human nature from favoring political supporters and punishing opponents? Can you imagine the layers of bureaucracy and impact of their stifling rules on productivity? Isn't this the realm of a moral society instead of authoritarian governments run by an elite few?

In Article 26, everyone has a right to free education, which is compulsory at the elementary level. How can it be free? Will teachers instruct for free? Who builds and maintains schools for nothing? Will classroom supplies also appear out of thin air? Obviously, people cannot work, build, or furnish for nothing, so government would have to force *someone* to toil without keeping the fruits of their labor in order to provide those positive "rights". We used to call that slavery.

As long as liberal globalists are generously dictating benefits across the continents, Article 27 announces that everyone has the right to enjoy the arts. A *right*? Then government must enforce it… with tickets to art galleries, concerts, and sports events that someone else pays for?

The U.N. did get one right correct: parents' right to choose the kind of education for their children. Obviously, the teachers' unions didn't have a say in that. Thankfully, the declaration also recognized in Article 29 that everyone has duties to the community. Notably, it didn't elaborate.

44 years later, the United Nations coordinated Agenda 21, a comprehensive, 351-page 1992 global action plan for the environment and development. It exhaustively identified goals, objectives, costs, as well as recommended donor nations. While its goals are lofty, it pays little attention to the primary institution that can affect change in developing nations: their governments.[17] Glaringly, there were no requirements for recipient countries to implement some form of "we the people-based" governance and socio-economic system in countries where prevailing ruinous dictatorships, monarchies, and communism act in opposition to Agenda 21's lofty goals.

Absent a radical change in government, culture, or human nature, do Agenda 21 adherents actually expect to achieve objective 3.7.a. in Saudi Arabia, "Empowering women through full participation in decision-making"? A worthy goal, but realistic? The list goes on.

What the plan *does* do is call on developed countries, primarily the United States, to pay the annual $600b that other countries cannot afford (that's 1992 dollars, or about $1.12 trillion today)[18]. The Plan's unquestioned and universal solution to other countries' plight, regardless of the efficacy and honesty of their governments, is a demand for more of someone else's resources (i.e., your family's). As an alternative approach, why aren't activists looking at how the U.S. became the most powerful, economically successful, and compassionate nation in just 244 years, then emulate those lessons of self-governance and open markets? That would produce more permanent change that permeates those societies, but is also much more challenging; starry-eyed activists seek the quick solution of throwing other people's money at the problems.

Significant national re-direction, as visioned in Agenda 21, have occurred. Consider the Scots' transition from poverty to international success. In the middle of the fifteenth century Scots were among the poorest and most ignorant people in Western Europe. Rather than perpetuate their past, leaders there decided to change – adopting English to avail themselves of its vast stores of knowledge and made significant advances in education, intellectual life, literature, art, architecture, music, politics, and science.

From this renaissance emerged Scottish steel magnate and philanthropist Andrew Carnegie; authors Robert Louis Stevenson, Sir Arthur Conan Doyle, Sir Walter Scott, and Robert Burns; surgeon James Braid; engineer James Watt (steam engine); telephone inventor Alexander Graham Bell; polar explorer William Bruce; pneumatic tire inventor Robert Thomson; economist Adam Smith; and Joseph Black – the father of quantitative chemistry. You already knew cinema's first James Bond was Scotsman Sean Connery, right?

6. **Climate.** "We, our children, and grandchildren are all going to horribly perish within a decade if we don't immediately start spending trillions of your earnings on our supporters' ideas to fight climate change!"

To gain attention and commitment to the more outrageous positions, liberals present them as apocalyptic world tragedies so epic that only [their] most enlightened candidates can possibly resolve them. For good measure, they heighten public fears by describing the most foreboding prophecies as existential.

Why should we be wary about their extreme climate claims? Look back about 15 years to Global Warming. That's when Democrat U.S. Vice President Al "I created the internet" Gore proposed to save the world from polar ice melt. A central component of his solution was a carbon exchange that operate like a commodities market. Companies that produced more carbon than government authorities allowed could use the exchange to purchase off-setting credits from companies that produced less than their allowance. It was vividly reminiscent of clerics in the Middle Ages collecting indulgences for a "get out of hell free" card to reduce eternal punishments for earthly sins.

During his Global Warming catastrophe speeches, Al neglected to mention his role as co-founder and CEO of carbon brokerage firm Generation Investment Management (GIM). Gore and his Goldman Sachs partner David Blood, of course, stood to reap significant financial rewards from its operation, especially if government *mandated* companies' participation.[19] Gore wouldn't respond to nationally-recognized investigative consumer reporter John Stossel's repeated invitations to debate with scientists who disagreed with him. Refusal to debate is always a red flag.

When a perpetrator hacked computers at Britain's University of East Anglia Climatic Research Unit in 2009, he (she?) posted emails between global warming scientists. The privileged communications immediately raised questions about the validity of the whole global warming narrative and coined the term "Climategate". What're proponents to do now?

Rebrand the cause! Shelve the sullied "Global Warming" title and re-brand it as "Climate Change". Now you can cover bets on both *hot and cold* weather, along with every hurricane, typhoon, and tornado! Brilliant, because the climate's always changing, right? The next step is tying climate changes to human activity and particularly to businesses (the bigger the better).

President Obama vigorously supported climate change programs during his eight years in office, but then bought a $15m Martha's Vineyard estate that's just feet above sea level. Isn't this staunch climate-change advocate concerned about rising ocean levels any more, or did he know it was just another mega-hoax all along?

In early 2019, U.S. Representative Alexandria Ocasio-Cortez (D-NY, a 26-year-old former bartender), and U.S. Senator Ed Markey, (D-MA) submitted identical versions of a Green New Deal (GND) resolution to their respective chambers.[20] She famously told us, "The world is going to end in 12 years if we don't address climate change." Their resolutions averred that human activity was the dominant cause of observed climate change over the past 100 years. As a direct result of that recklessness, they forecast that extreme weather would cause mass migrations, double the destruction due to wildfires, the loss of 99%+ of the earth's coral reefs, and more than 350,000,000 people being exposed to deadly heat.

I've Had Enough!

It went on to cite both pay and net worth differentials, crises in life expectancy, education, and wage stagnation, and threatened national security as further consequences of man-made climate change. My God, how are we to survive such existential calamities?

The World Meteorological Organization states that the global mean temperature for 2020 is 1.2 ± 0.1°C (2.2°F) above the 1850-1900 baseline used as an approximation of pre-industrial levels.[21] The U.S. National Oceanic and Atmospheric Administration reports that the global annual temperature has risen an average of 0.13° F per decade since 1880 and 0.32° F since 1981[22]; the UN forecasts another 2° - 5° increase this century. Former president of the American Association of State Climatologists and Senior Cato Institute Fellow Dr. Pat Michaels reflects that "…it's warmed up around 1° C since 1900, life expectancy doubled in the industrialized democracies, and yet that temperature ticks up another half a degree and the entire system crashes? That's the most absurd belief."[23]

Dr. Michaels went on to report that the Obama administration's climate model projected that the amount of global warming that would be saved if we magically achieved zero emissions would be an inconsequential 0.14° C.

Atmospheric physicist Richard Lindzen of the Massachusetts Institute of Technology explains that the scientists at the UN's International Panel on Climate Change believe CO_2 from burning fossil fuels may eventually dangerously heat the planet. Other scientists, himself included, disagree. A third group in the mix consists of politicians, environmentalists, media, and crony capitalists – each benefitting from doomsday scenarios and, unfortunately, drowning out serious debate.[24]

Notably, records at the U.S. National Oceanic and Atmospheric Administration's National Hurricane Center show no long-term increase in those storms' intensity.

Fortunately for the human race, Ocasio-Cortez and Markey emerged with solutions to their lethal forecasts, included dicta to eliminate all fossil fuels (especially tough to do with aircraft) in favor of clean, renewable, and zero-emission energy sources. They neglected to inform Americans that wind and solar power provide only about 3% of America's energy and physics limitations will preclude the geometric efficiency increases that the Green New Deal requires.

The GND and its zealots also neglect the environmental costs of converting an entire nation to wind and solar-generated electricity for the colossal waves of cars, trucks, trains, and every other electric-powered device. You may *feel* responsible driving an electric car until you realize the amount of coal or natural gas extracted and used to fuel the electric plant you're plugging in to. Batteries require additional excavation of earth's resources. There are *no* zero-emission energy sources when you consider what it takes to extract and refine raw materials, construct, maintain, and dispose of worn-out solar and wind farms and nuclear and hydroelectric facilities. Then there's the very considerable matter of electric energy storage and distribution. Examining such a massive tradeoff has considerable merit, but the GND doesn't begin to do that.

The GND goes on to insist on upgrading all buildings in the country to maximize energy and water efficiency, and expanding public transit and high-speed rail, perennial liberal darlings, despite their failures in the most liberal of our 50 states - CA. In February 2019, CA Governor Gavin Newsome pulled the plug on the state's liberal dream, a bullet train to connect Los Angeles and San Francisco. It was more than ten years behind schedule and billions of dollars in the red; the cold realities of supplying rail transit seats and enough demand for them to pay for exorbitant construction and operating costs exposed another liberal fantasy to the glaring light of reality.

Everyone's certainly in favor of a clean environment and healthy living conditions, and the resolution lays out some worthwhile goals. The GND, however, doesn't begin to consider their practicality or how to achieve most of them. Ironically, the Trump administration achieved two significant Green New Deal goals that the previous eight years of liberal leadership did not: stop the transfer of jobs overseas and grow domestic manufacturing.

In one final burst of naiveté, the document includes the goal of "...ensuring the use of... participatory processes... to implement... Green New Deal mobilization at the local level." Passage failed in the Senate 57-0; so much for crafting a bi-partisan plan acceptable to a single member of the majority party in that chamber.

Ocasio-Cortez apparently has very little appreciation for the costs and tradeoffs of the GND and appears oblivious to human nature. Co-sponsor Ed Markey should certainly know better.

7. **National Defense.** "OK, we may need *some* of it" liberals concede, "but what we have now is way too costly; it's nothing more than overstated hype that conservatives promote to benefit the military-industrial complex at the expense of the little people we champion. Besides, our so-called enemies are only reacting to American provocations and historical oppressions that we'll effectively deter through apologies and our much more sophisticated style of diplomacy."

Liberals don't comment on Russian President Vladimir Putin's overt seizure of the Crimea during President Obama's tenure. Nor do they discuss China's military build-up and warnings of possible military escalation after the UN's International Court of Justice firmly rejected the communist regime's territorial claims in the South China Sea. Given the Chinese Empire's past demands for tribute, regional countries have significant historical reason to be suspicious. China actively spars with India over their border. Do liberals also discount Chief of Naval Operations Admiral Gilday's October 2020 statement that "Specifically, China is the strategic threat to this country"?[25]

In October, China's recalcitrant communist neighbor, North Korea, unveiled what analysts believe is one of the world's largest intercontinental missiles, reportedly capable of reaching the U.S. mainland with multiple independent warheads. The Hermit Kingdom has also tested submarine-launched ballistic missiles. Will President Joe Biden resurrect Obama's "strategic patience" policy [i.e., do nothing] to safeguard us from those building threats?

Iran continues developing its own nuclear weapons, harasses maritime trade and oil exports through the critical Straits of Hormuz, and funds worldwide terrorists. The Liberal response? "Nothing to see here, keep moving, and watch those microaggressions. Can I tell you another bedtime story?"

8. Law enforcement is flagrantly racist and oppressive. "Uniformed, armed police are an unmitigated public evil (except for liberals' personal security details, of course). White supremacists have infiltrated their ranks to randomly and regularly hunt down, beat, and kill Blacks and other minorities at disproportionate rates to their population! Defund and immediately replace them with SWAT units [Social Workers And Therapists]!"

Utter nonsense. The first giveaway is citing "disproportionate rates" as proof of discrimination instead of explaining any actual causal factors. Activists in this arena fail to cite and substantiate their unfounded claims of racism across the millions of annual encounters between police and the public. A truth is that police do kill Blacks disproportionately more than their population, but Blacks also commit disproportionately more violent crimes - by a *very* large margin (see Chapters 10 and 11 for an in-depth review of the truth). Contrary to liberal sound bites, a summer 2020 Gallup poll found that 81% of black Americans said they'd like police to spend the *same or more* time in their neighborhoods.[26]

9. Sexual harassment and assault "We are proud, principled opponents of all forms of this kind of vile conduct. We ardently support the #MeToo movement... unless it involves one of our liberal candidates or elected officials like John and Ted Kennedy, Bill Clinton, John Edwards, Al Franken, Cal Cunningham, or Joe Biden. To prove how strongly we feel, we'll report 20-year-old events to block a Supreme Court confirmation and vow to prove the nominee's guilt even if he's confirmed."

The day the Senate *did* confirm Brett Kavanaugh as a Supreme Court Justice, progressives dropped the whole charade, never said another word about it.

Always willing to put image, votes, and power above propriety, Democrat presidential candidate Joe Biden made a well-publicized one-hour visit with the family of hospitalized black man

I've Had Enough!

Jacob Blake in Kenosha, WI. Police had charged Blake, already a charged with felony sexual assault, trespassing, and domestic abuse and there was an order restraining him from going to his victim's home. In violation of the order, Blake appeared at the victim's home. A neighbor called the police, who attempted to arrest him. Blake fought with the officers, then went to a vehicle and leaned in. One of them shot Blake multiple times; Blake survived.

Why didn't Biden visit the sexual assault victim? Or the officers who risked their lives to protect her and the neighborhood? Or proprietors whose businesses were burned by rioters after the incident? Nope, visiting a black felon generated much better headlines for the Black Lives Matter crowd.

10. **You have a right to healthcare**. "As the only compassionate political party, we hereby declare that everyone is entitled to this vital service for better living. And don't keep harping about who'll pay for it; we're a rich nation, so just write those damn checks to the IRS."

Libs know what a hot-button issue healthcare is, so in efforts to get electors' votes, obedience, and loyalty, they wrongfully tell voters it is their *right*. Recall that rights are promises the government is empowered and is responsible for enforcing. Notice too that liberals will never require their subjects to practice any personal behaviors to eat well, be active, and avoid risky conduct like smoking. Those requirements would entail personal responsibility, and liberals absolve you of that onerous obligation.

The only individual responsibility in President Obama's Affordable Care Act was to maintain coverage that liberals deemed sufficient (Americans paid a penalty if they didn't). The Obama administration and media misrepresented the program for the two years they developed it, telling Americans the penalties wouldn't be a tax... until they argued in front of the Supreme Court that they *were* a tax, which Congress had Constitutional authority to lay and raise.

Just like the open market raised the availability, quality, and affordability of services like long-distance telephone calls, can it do so with health care? Two measures would accelerate true competition and lower prices.

First, allow consumers to purchase insurance across state boundaries. Insurance has high economies of scale that individual states cannot provide. In 1944, when the health insurance industry was in its infancy, the Supreme Court ruled that the federal government would be responsible for regulating the insurance industry. That same year, however, crony capitalism crept into the equation with the McCarran-Ferguson Act. It deregulated federal authority back to the states, and many of those governments restricted consumers to buying in-state-policies (from companies that supported lawmakers' restrictive legislative efforts).

A 2008 Department of Health and Human Services study estimated that just over 12 million previously uninsured people would have coverage if consumers could shop coverage and premiums nationally.[27]

The second action is one of transparency: requiring health care facilities to make available on the internet and lobby displays the outcomes and average and highest charges for the 50 most frequently-performed procedures over the past 12 months. They should also display their infection rates. The Centers for Disease Control (CDC) should make performance data available on its web site down to individual health care facility-level rather than just to state level. Currently, you can find information about individual participating healthcare facilities at TheLeapfrogGroup.org; it would be a useful model for a more expansive source of information.

Both of these implementations would make healthcare insurance more competitive – driving down prices while still offering better service.

11. **National borders are needless and hateful.** "Hey, people, it's one big planet, right? Who are we to deny fellow humans from coming to this part of it? With us liberals in charge, the USA is open to everyone who wants to come here – just saunter on in, whether you're skilled, unskilled, infected, or a criminal. There's certainly no need to go through discriminatory naturalization processes that white racist European males devised. If you vote Democrat, we'll make other family budgets pay for your health care,

education, housing, food, and we'll even let you vote in our most progressive states. We're doing it, of course, to help the world's impoverished people."

Really? Their solution to the world's poverty-stricken is for all of them to come to the U.S.? The World Bank estimates the number of people in 2020 who are in extreme poverty (under $1.90/day) will be 40m – 60m. Those living on less than $3.20 a day could rise to 40m – 150m, and people living on less than $5.50/day may rise as high as 180m. With our population standing at about 330 million, there is no way to support and assimilate half that number again into our intricate society. Any significant increase in the current 1 million annual legal immigrants raises unanswered considerations of their impact on infrastructure (schools, healthcare, housing, and the like) and competition for jobs that our own poor need.

Increasing liberals' political power base looms as a much stronger motivation than compassion for liberal leaders' immigration and border policy efforts.

We also have to ask whether we're helping or hurting the worldwide humanitarian effort when we accept many of the most energetic, brightest, and motivated from struggling countries. How would their lost talents and ideas negatively impact the nations they leave?

12. **A job with a livable wage.** "Everyone needs a job that pays enough to live in dignity. Since it's a need, it must also be a government-enforced right, right? Of course, we liberals will determine how high a wage businesses will have to pay, regardless of how little your skills contribute to production or whether you work at all. Remember, we're just demonstrating our compassion."

Needs are *not* rights. Everyone *needs* food, clothing, shelter, and health care, but has no *right* to force others to provide them. We are individually responsible for providing for our needs by earning the means to do so in the marketplace. When people are unable to provide for their basic needs, family, faith, service, and charitable organizations are called upon to provide those needs through a sense of moral responsibility, but not under a government threat.

"Livable wage" campaigners often point out the pay difference between the lowest worker in a company and its chief, "A General Motors assembler making $16.52 and hour would have to work 64 years to equal the CEO's annual $2.1m salary. It's criminal!" They never ever ask how many years it'd take the assembler to successfully guide the corporation through worldwide markets, legal hurdles, and capricious consumers with many other options. Nor do livable wage reformists calculate how many years it'd take an assembler to manage the corporation's value through new products, stock sales and purchases as GM's CEO Mary Marra has done. Likewise, activists don't consider the relative impact of mistakes made by an assembler and the CEO.

Ultra-liberal 2020 presidential candidate Bernie Sanders vociferously campaigned that we're such a rich country that we can afford for everyone to have a "livable income and retire in dignity". He failed to explain that the country is rich because of our open market economy that compensates so many individuals who adhere to productive behaviors (detailed in Chapter 15).

13. **Voter suppression** "This heinous conservative tactic denies liberals (especially minorities) the right to cast ballots. Those preposterous, racist conservatives actually insist on picture IDs to vote!"

Liberals broadcast this tripe every election to smear legitimate and necessary measures to ensure the integrity of fair elections. Given the dynamics of voter moves between jurisdictions and states, officials have the responsibility to ensure voter rolls are accurate. Ditto for clearing deceased voters and ineligible persons (such as felons) from the rolls. We expect poll workers to uphold process integrity by confirming people obtaining a ballot are actually on the voter rolls; John Gates Smith must be matched with John Gates Smith, not with his neighbor John Bates Smith or John Gates Smyth.

Stacy Abrams, 2018 Georgia candidate for governor, is the poster child for this tactic. When she lost by 55,000 votes (1.4% of ballots cast), she proclaimed election fraud due to voter suppression.

I've Had Enough!

Fellow lib and presidential candidate Pete Buttigieg quickly chimed in, "Racially motivated patterns of voter suppression are responsible for Stacey Abrams not being governor of Georgia right now."

Never miss a chance to interject some racial tension, and be sure to vote progressive Democrat to eradicate all those pesky checks and balances.

14. **We love you**. "While Republicans, conservatives, and entitled Whites have a disdain or even hatred for people (especially, women and minorities), *we're* the ones who really care about you. Everyone who doesn't agree with us is racist and only cares about profits. If you're Black, we *really* love you during election season; we and the professors are still working on a plan that does something for you in between elections. Trust us... again, and again, and again."

Yes, some liberal efforts have helped those with no voice, but conservatives have too. The Grand Old Party (GOP) was literally founded as the anti-slavery political party. See Chapter 5 for Congressional conservatives' much more enthusiastic support of the 1964 Civil Rights Act, the 1965 Voter Rights Act, and the 1968 Fair Housing Act.

15. **Instant gratification.** "Everyone's entitled to it - immediate fulfillment of their feelings, wants, needs, and expectations, no matter how shallow, illogical, expensive, and fanciful. You millennials listen up: no entry-level grunt work to learn the ropes when *we're* in charge; no siree – an instant managerial position with high five-figure salary, Cadillac health plan, one-month vacation, and a generous annual bonus!"

The first lesson of economics is scarcity: there is never enough of anything to fully satisfy all those who want it. The first lesson of politics is to disregard the first lesson of economics.

Thomas Sowell

Absent the hype from politicians, mature adults know there's no free lunch. It often takes time, experience, and some bumps along the way to become proficient in your field. The siren song of instant gratification is alluring, but it's a childish appeal whose proponents know better.

16. "You absolutely have the right to **not be offended.** No one has any right to offend you through their insensitive political positions, beliefs, speech, dress, personal grooming, or any other way you can dream up that you deem inappropriate or makes you feel uncomfortable or excluded. We good liberals are here to aggressively persecute anyone who violates this sacred right - unless you're a conservative who's offended by our fellow liberals!"

Not so, not by a long shot. Yes, it's unseemly to knowingly offend others, but there's certainly and absolutely no *right* to not be offended. This is particularly true when delicate senses feel offended by the slightest action or conversation. If you're offended, consider the source and disregard it for the objectionable element you deem it to be.

Liberals are steeped in these beliefs and fervently advocate them at every opportunity: marches, demonstrations, riots, newscasts, interviews, proclamations, facebook pages, tweets, and blogs. They infuse them into courses in elementary, middle, and high schools and most colleges. In August, 2020, Iowa State Professor Chloe Clark didn't even hide her ultra-liberal prejudices; her syllabus included the following threat:[28]

"GIANT WARNING: Any instances of othering that you participate in intentionally (racism, sexism, ableism, homophobia, sorophobia, transphobia, classism, mocking of mental health issues, body shaming, etc.) in class are grounds for dismissal from the classroom,"

Administrators only forced the prejudiced liberal professor to amend her entry rather than promptly terminating the narrow-minded faculty member who *should* be encouraging diversity of thoughts and require solid arguments to support them.

In a final test of practicality and accommodation of human nature, ask what societies that've enacted the liberal-progressive manifesto has survived, significantly raised its members' overall standard of living, and become the beacon for the rest of the world?
I'll wait.

Chapter 4: The Liberal Game Plan

H aving blissfully decided their ultimate objective and positions, liberals have devised, refined, and routinely practice strategies and tactics to control people, governments, and public and private wealth. In attempts to legitimize their positions, they create moral justifications that are fervently presented with impassioned conviction but thin on truth. Here are their primary strategies.

1. Divide and Conquer

Reproduced with the generous permission of Dave Coverly, speedbump.com

This strategy could just as well be titled "Divide, *Discriminate*, and Conquer", because that's exactly what happens when you stoke and mobilize resentment to get what you want. Liberals have long recognized the advantages of sowing discontent to disrupt unity of thought, values, and effort and they employ the tactic shamelessly. They've developed several perpetual activities to foster division and subversion, then promote themselves as saviors of downtrodden women, black people and other minorities (just before an election), morality (if you can believe that), and everything right-eous.

Where consensus is on the rise, they fan the embers of dis-sention and add kindling. Where people are progressing as individuals or as a community, they'll research and reignite past feuds or merrily instigate new ones. "It is up to us to go in and rub raw the sores of discontent" urged Saul Alinsky, author of *Rules for Radicals,* a fundamental guide for left-wing activists the subject of Hillary Rodham [Clinton]'s Wellesley senior thesis.

Far-leftists don't seek or trumpet true national unity, but are quick to spotlight and dwell on differences with gut-level childish appeals that're easily expressed on a bumper sticker ("Trump killed 220,000 people!). They go on to link those differences to opponents and repeatedly tell the divided group how none of it's their fault, "The reason you're not rich is because "they" took advantage of you; our political enemies victimized you."

In August 2020, Democrat CA Governor Gavin Newsome criticized the President for contributing to the state's annual rash of wild fires because the President didn't support liberals' climate change agenda. Newsome neglected to comment on how the state did (or more accurately didn't) control dense underbrush on state lands, incidents of arson, and fires from faulty Pacific Gas and Elec-tric utility equipment.

A subset of the Divide and Conquer tactic is denigrating high achievers, which plays out particularly well because it relies on peo-ple's innate envy of other's income and/or wealth. It's a perennial liberal power play to *gain* advantage by *taking* advantage of voters' human nature – preying on their instinct to protect their sense of self-worth by shifting their failures to others instead of recognizing and curing their own shortfalls.

Think about it; everybody knows someone making more money than they do and who *certainly* doesn't deserve that much. The libs purposely don't define how much makes you "rich" be-cause doing so would establish a specific threshold. Much more politically expedient to let everyone, even comfortably-entrenched middle-class voters, form their *own* opinion of how much income is too much and conclude "That rich SOB is making more than I do", when they themselves are "the rich SOB" to others.

Loosely and frequently spouting terms like millionaires and billionaires adds fuel to the fire and garners additional sympathizers for liberal candidates eagerly posing as "champions of the little people." Incidentally, liberal apparatchiks dropped the term "millionaires" from the 2020 race for the Democrat presidential nomination when voters discovered the vast majority of *their own* candidates were millionaires or multimillionaires.

The punitive costs of liberal socialism and attacking high achievers in New York are reaching a climax there, prompting Democrat New York Governor Andrew Cuomo in August 2020 to announce that, "A single percent of New York's population pays *half* the state's taxes, and they're the most mobile people on the globe. You've got to come back! We'll go out to dinner! I'll buy you a drink! Come over, I'll cook!"

"Soak the rich!" is their unbroken battle cry to rally supporters who think, "That makes sense, they make more than I do so they should pay more." Just how much *do* "the rich" make and pay in federal income taxes?

The IRS reports that the top 5% of earners had adjusted gross incomes comprising 34% of the nation's total individual income in 2017. They paid, however, *56%* of the nation's individual income taxes – well over half. No such illuminations ever cross a campaigning liberal's lips, and certainly not after they're in office.

What do rich people actually *do* with their wealth? We immediately think of posh lifestyles of mansions, exotic cars, designer clothes, jewelry, gala events, five-star dining, and first-class travel. When they do spend that way, the expenses are incomes to architects, builders, craftsmen, landscapers, laborers, engineers, mechanics, and finishers who build, sell, repair, and maintain their estate, yacht, airplane, and exotic cars. The rich's expenses also pay wages to their suppliers, delivery drivers, caterers, entertainers, and servers who cater events. The rich ultimately pay the wages of those who process raw materials into metals, cloths, finished woods, and other components, laborers sub-contractors,

OK, so how about just imposing a luxury tax on their goodies; the government "recovers" more of their ill-gotten gains *and* the downstream workers still have their jobs! Not so, as the Clinton administration discovered: when you go after all those expensive toys, people stop buying them and you also put the toymakers and their elves out of business.

When less ostentatious rich Americans save their earnings instead of spending them, banks have more money to lend to borrowers pursuing their ideas and dreams – a home or car, kids' education, starting their own business, medical bills, you name it.

Still other wealthy individuals and couples decide to invest their loot. They didn't get rich by being dumb, so they seek profitable investments with promising new ideas in technology, manufacturing, health, and the like. No investors, no progress there.

What else can they do with their wealth? They can donate it, which enables organizations like the Bill and Melinda Gates Foundation to use $48b to fund education, lift people out of poverty all over the world, and eradicate worldwide malaria and polio. In May 2020 that organization committed another $250m to support research, development, and delivery of COVID-19 vaccines. Damn those rich people!

None of those benefits accruing to ordinary folks support the liberal narrative, so you'll never hear their mainstream media partners report them. You *will* hear the repetitive message that all wealthy people made their wealth on the backs of you voters. That presupposes that rich people somehow took an outsized grab from a fixed-sized community pot of money – which is absurd. Many rich people created brand new wealth from completely new ideas like UBER, Tesla, Facebook, Apple, and Amazon.

Another favorite term that rolls off liberals' tongues is "fair share", as in "Elect us to make corporations pay their fair share of taxes." They never compare our corporate tax rate to other countries' rates. Until the Trump administration reduced the federal corporate tax rate, the U.S. rate was higher than Europe's and Asia's – making it much tougher for our companies to compete and retain American workers.

Business owners and managers are regular targets because everyone knows the boss and his do-nothing, white-collar cronies get paid more than you do, right? President Obama took a podium in Virginia to stoke the crowd's animosity, exasperation, and the envy he was anxious to harness, "If you've got a business, you didn't build that. Someone else made that happen,"[29] The unspoken message was, "They got there and get paid more by taking advantage of you. That's wrong, it's immoral, and I'm going to fix it; vote for me!" That said, it's not only a gut-satisfying course of action, but one that's now presumably couched in morality.

Of course, Obama neglected to tell audiences that workers have the freedom to leave employers and that businesses pay considerable taxes in support of public infrastructure like roads and schools. His gullible voters didn't think about those truths.

The President also neglected to mention what those "filthy entrepreneurs" *did* do. They had an idea and the tenacity to pursue it. They took substantial risks to make their dream a reality. And remember, there's absolutely *no guarantee* that people will decide to buy their products or services, and the whole business could go belly-up. Wage earners work a fixed number of hours and leave the job behind when they clock out. Entrepreneurs and leaders, on the other hand, are working as long as it takes - until 10:00 pm or 12:00 am. While workers routinely cash their payroll checks, many small business owners have to assume a second mortgage to make the month's payroll and they take a reduced or no salary themselves. Their businesses also pay hefty taxes to support the infrastructure they rightfully use.

Liberal campaigns also divide us through the use of folksy keywords, like *Native American* and *indigenous people*. Apparently, they and their supporters don't realize that everyone born in the United States is a native, indigenous American. The earliest immigrants who preceded Europeans in North America arrived from Asia via the Bering Strait with their own expansionist goals. In this regard, they were little if any different from rival tribes and settlers who followed them.[30] Present day Texas saw millennia of conquests by Pueblos, Jumanos, Caddos, Karankawas, Apaches and other Plains tribes, Spanish conquistadores, French, Spanish again, and Mexicans before the final victors, Texans, prevailed.

By 1750, the Comanches kept the Cheyenne at bay farther north of the Comancheria empire and rid it of Pawnees, Utes,

I've Had Enough!

Osages, Blackfeet, Kiowas, Apaches, and Tonkawas. U.S. Army units, in turn, defeated the Comanches.

Before Europeans battled the Iroquois, the Iroquois destroyed the Huron and Erie tribes during their westward movement to the Ohio Valley in the 1600s.

President Mirabeau Buonaparte Lamar of the Republic of Texas launched an 1839 campaign against Indians that was more immoral than treatment of Blacks during Reconstruction. Unlike slaves who'd never owned land, tribes in east Texas had peacefully worked their own farms for years when Lamar's army wholesale killed Cherokees, Delawares, Shawnees, Caddoans, Kickapoos, Muskogees, and Seminoles in east Texas and burned their villages to ashes.

Another divisive liberal moniker is *African American.* Rather than simply and accurately state they're talking about people with dark skin, the politically correct crowd avoids reality by referring to them by the geographical origin of many of their great, great, great, great ancestors – Africa.

Do they realize that any number of other Americans can be from Africa too, including Egyptians, other Arabs, even Whites from South Africa? Liberals simply cannot bring themselves to overtly distinguish people by skin color ("How racist!"), so they created the illusory nomenclature of "African American". If we categorize people by the continent some early ancestor lived in and the continent they're currently in, wouldn't it be proper to refer to Blacks here as African-North Americans so they're not confused with African-Latin Americans, African-Central Americans, and African-South Americans?

To further demonstrate the absurdity of PC identity games, recognize that anthropologists report that *everyone* can ultimately trace their origins back to the Dark Continent, so we're *all* African-Americans under liberal logic.[31] How many generations must pass from those bygone roots before today's descendants are known simply as Americans? It's ridiculous.

2. Regulate Lives Through Extensive Government Control

Life in general has never been even close to fair, so the pretense that

R.J. Ross

the government can make it fair is a valuable and inexhaustible asset
to politicians who want to expand government.

Thomas Sowell

Liberals believe they are the exclusive fountain of knowledge when it comes to running a society and every individual in it: how to raise and educate your children, who should be admitted to college regardless of academic preparation, what constitutes a government-enforceable right that infringes on other people's rights, how much you should earn and what is too much – the list of intrusions is sweeping.

Sure, some ideas make sensible goals, but decisions to embrace them in our republic are *individual* decisions. Does it make sense to ride a motorcycle without wearing a helmet? Most people don't think so. Others, though, weigh the risk of a head injury against the unencumbered thrill of wind in their face and make the opposite decision. Ditto for skydivers, bungee-jumpers, deep sea divers, citizens who enlist in the military and police departments, firemen, and numerous other pursuits. Many a concert goer is happy to enjoy loud music now rather than preserve their hearing for later years, and millions of Americans still smoke, chew tobacco, drink sugar-laden beverages, and freely eat large frequent servings of fried food.

When enough of the population doesn't accept their ideas, staunch liberals turn to government to impose their philosophy through force. The Affordable Care Act, popularly referred to as Obama Care, is a prime example that affected the entire population.

NYC's liberal Mayor Bloomberg went so far as to ban the sale of many 16 oz or larger sweetened drinks; fortunately, the NY Court of Appeals overturned his liberal overreach.

To manage so many aspects of our personal and working lives, liberals readily create new government departments and expand those in existence. And every new bureaucrat comes at a price – which tax-paying Americans are compelled to fund instead of buying food, clothing, a home improvement, school for the kids, a vacation, or saving for retirement.

I've Had Enough!

3. Communications

"To learn who rules over you, simply find out who you are not allowed to criticize."

Voltaire

The astounding ability of social media to rapidly connect billions of people throughout the world is absolutely unprecedented.[2] That, of course, makes them gold mines for business and priceless diamond mines for those eager to shape or re-shape political opinions.

Consequently, the sites' leaders are faced with some tough issues: which postings do they allow, promote, censor, or outright prohibit? Who decides what criteria to use to answer those questions and how have they applied them? How do leaders simultaneously uphold American principles of free speech and avoid political favoritism? With some 222m U.S. facebook users alone, the public and all sides of the political spectrum are intent on knowing how successful they those leaders are on all these critical issues.

Those sites and the major liberal newspapers and broadcast media uniformly denigrated, suppressed or gave scant coverage to the conservative president's major accomplishments, destroying ISIS, achieving energy independence, lowest recorded unemployment rates for Blacks, women, and Hispanics, driving accelerated COVID-19 vaccine development, normalization of diplomatic relations between Israel and three Muslim Mid East countries, lowered corporate and individual income taxes, secure the southern border, negotiate more balanced trade agreements with China, Mexico, and Canada, create the Space Force and enhance our existing military services.

The Ellis Island Honors Society awarded Donald J. Trump, alongside Rosa Parks and Muhammad Ali, its Ellis Island Medal of Honor, recognized by both the U.S. House of Representatives and

---

[2] Includes Facebook, Instagram, Twitter, and Snapchat

46

Senate, for their contributions to civil rights.[32] the Ali Foundation itself honored Trump at their annual gala dedicated to recognizing "people who are making significant contributions toward securing peace, social justice and/or human rights."

Those are monumental achievements, especially by a first-time elected official in his first term, that warrant more thorough coverage.

In an analysis of coverage of ABC, CBS and NBC evening newscasts during June and July 2020, the Media Research Center found 8 positive and 4 negative statements about liberal presidential candidate Joe Biden vs. 34 positive and 634 negative statements about the conservative president.[33] Liberal-leaning on-line news-feeds retain on their front pages negative stories about conservatives.

Those media simultaneously overlooked significant negative stories about the liberal candidate, such as his recorded threat to withhold U.S. money from Ukraine unless that country's president immediately terminated a special prosecutor investigating the sena-tor's son for illegal activities there. In October 2020, the New York Post, founded 220 years ago by Founding Father Alexander Hamil-ton, ran a front-page story about incriminating material found on a laptop computer linked to Democrat presidential-nominee Joe Biden's son. Facebook limited the spread of the story and Twitter blocked users' posts about the story altogether. Both cited concerns over sharing material that may be hacked or personal. They had ab-solutely no such concerns during the two-year investigations into a collusion hoax aimed at the sitting conservative president.

More recently, on January 6, 2021 tens of thousands of pres-idential supporters filled some 45 acres of space between the Ellipse and the Washington Monument. They'd come from states near and far to hear his 70-minute-long remarks at the Save America March gathering. The president enumerated a number of specific examples of election issues in key states where he'd been leading by comfort-able margins but were later certified in favor of his opponent. During his remarks he prevailed on the vice president to send the electoral results back to those states to re-vote and ended with encouraging words for the country's future.

I've Had Enough!

Immediately afterwards, a much smaller contingent moved to the U.S. Capitol and some of those breached police barricades, entered the building, and participated in acts of vandalism. Investigations are ongoing to determine who the criminals were and their political motivations (Trump supporters? ANTIFA? BLM?). Tragically, police fatally shot one woman and three people later died who suffered medical emergencies. Twitter and Facebook temporarily suspended the president's accounts, claiming he was spreading dangerous misinformation and encouraging violence.[34] Curiously, their concerns about years of spreading dangerous information and encouraging violence surrounding justifiable high-profile police killings fell must have under different guidelines.

Two days later, the president broadcast two tweets:

"The 75,000,000 great American Patriots who voted for me, AMERICA FIRST, and MAKE AMERICA GREAT AGAIN, will have a GIANT VOICE long into the future. They will not be disrespected or treated unfairly in any way, shape or form!!!"

"To all of those who have asked, I will not be going to the Inauguration on January 20th."

Twitter quickly announced, "After close review of recent Tweets from the @realDonaldTrump account and the context around them we have permanently suspended the account due to the risk of further incitement of violence."[35]

The media giant construed that the first message could be viewed as a further statement that the election was not legitimate and may incite violence. Paradoxically, Twitter did not suspend accounts of reporters who cited the president's exact same words. One wonders if they fancied the second tweet a veiled invitation for inaugural violence since the president wouldn't be there?

Facebook's CEO said its block would remain in place through the end of the president's term and potentially indefinitely.[36] Given the gravity of their discussions, one wonders if there were any contrasting speakers at the tables to voice other perspectives and how those media's actions would impact the broader principle of free speech.

Print and broadcast media immediately labeled the president's remarks sedition and urged the vice president to lead the cabinet in removing the president for an inability to perform his duties, as provided under the 25th Amendment. The vice president did not and the Democratic-majority house and filed a single article of impeachment on Jan 11 for the crime of incitement of insurrection.

In light of growing actions against conservatives, many of them dumped their Facebook accounts and turned to another social media site – Parlor. Apple Computer promptly dropped the conservative-leaning app site from its store and Amazon suspended its hosting service for the app (Amazon CEO Jeff Bezos also owns the Washington Post). Both cited concerns about members spreading violence, but took no similar actions against facebook and twitter for consistently allowing Black Lives Matter and other liberal organizations' narratives about "police murders" that incited violence for years.

4. Control Education

"The problem isn't that Johnny can't read. The problem isn't even that Johnny can't think. The problem is that Johnny doesn't know what thinking is; he confuses it with feeling."

Thomas Sowell

How would families react if grocery, clothing, and department stores forced customers to shop at only one of their many outlets? Customers would be rightly baffled, outraged, and repudiate the decree. Yet, that's exactly what so many parents blindly accept from local school boards that draw boundaries dictating the single government school their children must attend.

The one factor all government schools share is staffing by loyal unionized government teachers whose considerable dues fund campaigns to keep compliant officials in power to protect their jobs and pay.[37]

Liberals refuse to consider parental school choice through the use of vouchers that parents could apply towards private school tuition, and they routinely object to charter schools. They never emphasize family obligations to create and sustain the culture of education that many Asian families do very successfully. Nor do they insist that students attend class, behave, participate, and do their homework ("What? Act White and betray my race?").

Wholesale student failures to achieve reading, writing, and math standards practically never lead to teachers' dismissals, but become a clarion call to raise taxes for more teachers or higher salaries and more iPads. New York City employs about 79,000 teachers, of whom only 15 were fired, and those were from a pool of 237 misconduct cases.[38]

Liberal personalities are drawn to the field of education, and once there, they infuse the group-think gospel of "How does it make you *feel?*" into absorbing minds from elementary school through post-graduate level. They demonize free markets and omit their success in raising the standard of living for people more than any socialist or communist system ever has. They neglect references to socialism/communism's murderous worldwide failures throughout history. Individual responsibility is relegated to a back burner without a flame.

At liberal colleges and universities, administrators employ every ploy, practice, and fabrication to admit less-academically prepared black and Hispanic applicants over many Asians and Whites. Liberals throughout California's university system are legendary for their efforts to skirt the state's constitutional amendment 209 prohibiting race when considering admissions.

Once admitted to schools with the most demanding student requirements, affirmative action students as a group do poorer academically, switch to less-demanding (and lower-paying) majors, or fail completely. Those students would have a better chance of succeeding if they'd attended schools more closely aligned with their academic preparation.

After admissions, universities can lower the goal posts in other ways, too. The Rutgers Graduate Writing Program that advises students on writing their dissertations evaluates them either "Satisfactory or Unsatisfactory; satisfactory performance is largely determined by attendance and engagement."[39] The Chairwoman of Rutgers University's Department of English seems to have prioritized students' casual grammar over established rules that more accurately convey ideas to diverse audiences. Time will tell how the deviations designed to "advantage multi-lingual and "non-standard" English speakers" affects differing interpretations of contracts, scientific papers, laws, and the like. It sounds an awful lot like PC code for accommodating students who are academically unprepared for that renowned university's rigors.

Administrations and students alike contrive a distorted, self-serving illusion of threats to designate and prohibit unfavorable ideas as "hate speech". When students arrive on many campuses, they find that officials suppress truth and intellectual challenge by establishing physical "safe zones" that restrict dissenting voices to small, obscure, "free speech zones". Pierce College in Los Angeles established a free speech zone about the size of three parking spaces. In 2016, Student Kevin Shaw challenged the limitation and prevailed; the LA Community College District then abandoned its declaration that all of its nine campuses were "non-public forums." [40]

The insidious techniques go on and on: present only conforming opinions and writings; vigorously exclude speakers with different ideas - to the extent of physically attacking and blocking them and audiences from venues.[41] Administrators and faculty join the cordons right beside the student thought-police. After the intellectual embargo, liberal faculty members goose-step back to the classroom and pander to the budding 'scholars' self-declared fears and rights.

College instructors and administrators encourage and fully support too many self-absorbed, narcissistic students claiming membership in ever smaller and more exclusive groups that demand special protection from their neurotic phobias. Are they trembling from widespread campus beatings, manslaughter, and murders? Hardly.

In March 2016, Emory University sophomore Jonathon Peraza and a handful of fellow students sought a meeting with university President Jim Wagner, which he eventually granted. Peraza told Wagner of their "pain at seeing pro-Trump graffiti written in chalk on a sidewalk". What? Pain at seeing a chalked name?

I've Had Enough!

Initially refusing to meet student demands to send out a school-wide email, Wagner caved that night and validated the students' obsessive victimhood and paranoia by swearing to "...effect immediate refinements to certain policy and procedural deficiencies...". Like what? The same year Peraza was fearfully trembling over chalked "Trump" writings, Emory University reported *no* on-campus student housing murders or manslaughter, one aggravated assault, 3 rapes and 10 burglaries among their 14,000+ student population.[42]

Compare Peraza's cowering character and demeanor with the leadership of Todd Beamer and 39 other unarmed civilians aboard flight 93 on 9/11. They revolted against Al-Qaeda hijackers to prevent the four terrorists from flying the plane into the U.S. Capitol. Well, actually, you can't; there's absolutely no comparison between them.

In contrast to Emory University's President Wagner, Oklahoma Wesleyan University President Dr. Everett Piper took an adult approach. When a student complained to a senior faculty member that he felt "victimized" and uncomfortable from a Sunday service reading of 1 Corinthians 13, Piper also sent a statement to the student body. His ended with the reality, "This is not a day care. This is a university." Amen! (Oops, today's libs would say Awomen.

The real threat in a liberal or any other supremacy isn't the 10% who are true believers and profiteers, it's the other 90% who mindlessly accept and act upon their narratives.

5. Redefine Language and Culture

"He who dares not offend cannot be honest."

Thomas Paine

The liberal campaign marches on to outright change and obfuscate language and marginalize or ignore facts, truths, and history. The obscuring fog of "Political Correctness" reigns supreme, with the term itself a ruse. "Correct" is comporting with fact and reason, not just enabling social or political objectives.

If illegal aliens are "undocumented immigrants", are drug dealers merely undocumented pharmacists, and shoplifters are "non-paying customers"? Some elected liberal officials are claiming that

52

looted goods aren't stolen property, but simply reparations. New York Times bestselling author Michelle Alexander now refers to ex-felons as "formerly incarcerated" or "returning citizens" in some hope no one will ask, "Incarcerated... for what?" or "Returning from where, a Caribbean cruise?" Like the movie *Stonehurst Asylum*, the patients have taken over the institution.

Switching the word order of adjectives and nouns is a liberal favorite that's somehow supposed to completely change who they're talking about. We no longer have "colored people", but "people of color". Inexplicably, any prejudice, undertones, or nuances associated with someone or something described with an adjective-noun word order magically evaporates by the reversal. Do wooden tables now become tables of wood? Such is the liberal thought process.

Even though the Merriam-Webster dictionary defines "Oriental" as "of, relating to, or coming from Asia and especially eastern Asia", the PC crowd has resolved that it can describe art or food, but it's now offensive when referring to people. Go figure... Regardless of the word order, Asians /Orientals apparently do not have a color, since liberals routinely exclude them from discussions about "people of color" when it comes to educational accomplishments, income, and crime rates. But why should they exclude this visually distinct and historically oppressed racial minority that's thrived in the land of opportunity rather than bemoan a victimhood status like a number of Blacks do?

In a similar linguistic sleight-of-hand, the liberal intelligentsia have jettisoned the noun "homosexual" (literally "same sex") and replaced it with "gay" (which meant happy or light hearted before liberals redefined it). Many libs today don't even recognize the fundamental binary genders of male and female, but demand universal recognition of people's daily emotional definition of their gender. One reference lists 112 such self-identified classifications.[43] Whatever mental mix of behaviors thoughts, and feelings people hold is their business, but it doesn't come close to turning biology on its head and forcing everyone else to play along.

The liberal gender crowd also wants the world to suddenly join their fantasy of making plural pronouns refer to the singular. Depending on how you imagine your gender one day, they demand that you refer to a single female, for example, as "they" or "them" instead of the correct singular words she or her.

Sound other-worldly? Nope, it's absolute reality in the liberals' world of cultural change. NYC's Commission on Human Rights' 2015 guidelines plainly legislates that the Commission can impose civil penalties of up to *$250,000* if it deems your failure to use someone's preferred pronoun or title is "willful, wanton, or malicious conduct".[44] Be warned: if you willfully address someone with proper English that doesn't conform with their delusion, take out your checkbook. No more First Amendment in the liberal's NYC, just more patients in the asylum's front office.

University of Michigan junior Grant Strobl demonstrated the idiocy of the liberal pronoun craze in 2016 when he responded to the school's Designated Pronoun policy. He chose the title "His Majesty" to showcase how ridiculous the policy was and its utter detachment from reality.[45] What if you identify as a goat tomorrow? Or better yet, as a lamb so "ewe" can shower with the coeds? You'll have to clear it with proponents Provost Martha Pollack and VP of Academic Affairs E. Royster Harper.

Resisting such absurdity, Professor Nicholas Meriwether filed a federal lawsuit against Shawnee State University after he was formally disciplined for not acceding to a male student's demand to be addressed in class as a woman. He'd agreed to call the student by his first or last name, but not to bow to a whimsical lexicon rooted in a liberal illusion. Bill Clinton-appointed federal judge Susan Dlott dismissed the case. Thus, language is redefined.

The 3+ million-member National Education Association and others now uses the invented term Latinx to describe combinations of both male and female Hispanics (where Spanish has used Latino and Latina since the language's origin). Even though most Hispanics don't use the term themselves, how long will it before liberals ban entire languages that are sexist – like Latin, French, German, Spanish, and Italian, which all assign gender to many of their words?

Fabricated "gender-neutral" pronouns now include zi, zir, zem, zeir, xe, xir, xem, and xeir. Does Michigan mix zi and xe roommates in dormitory room assignments? Once graduated, is it possible to claim a gender pay-difference between people who proclaim gender neutrality?

In the newsroom, the Associated Press decided to capitalize the word "black" when used as the name of a race, but not do so with "white". They rationalized the flagrantly discriminatory double standard out of fear that "White" would subtly lend an air of legitimacy to white supremacists. What? Who dreams this crap up? Apparently, the AP wizards didn't consider that "Black" may also lend a subtle air of legitimacy to the violent, revolutionary socialist Black Panthers organization founded by Marxist students Bobby Seale and Huey Newton. Maybe the AP liberals also overlooked "lending an air of legitimacy" to the New Black Panther Party for Self Defense, which the Southern Poverty Law Center describes as "... a bigoted, anti-white, anti-Semitic Black Nationalist group that preaches hate toward the LGBT and Jewish communities...".

Note: I follow the practice of capitalizing both nouns Black and White as names of races, and use lower case "black" and "white" for adjectives, as in black man or white culture.

You'll see libs refer to their preferred health care program as "single payer." The term actually describes a coveted federally-run system; another progressive subterfuge to replace open markets with ever more socialism.

Liberals are also prone to employ presentism - using today's standards to judge past leaders and events. They relish evaluating past figures by the nadir or a single event in their lives and destroying any heritage that doesn't conform to their manifesto. By such a standard, should we topple Dr. Martin Luther King statues and rename parks and street signs bearing his name for his plagiarism in academic papers and legion infidelities?[46] Rename Harvard's JFK School of Government due to John Kennedy's famous philandering?

Of course, it goes without saying that principled liberals have to topple the West Virginia State Capitol statue of former Senator Robert C. Byrd (D-WV) and eradicate his name from Shepard University's Center for Congressional History and Education. While you're at it, remove his name from Biotechnology Science Center and Center for Rural Health at Marshall University due to his role as a KKK Exalted Cyclops and filibustering against the 1964 Civil Rights Act.[47]

I've Had Enough!

In a letter to fellow Klansman and Senator Theodore Bilbo (D-MS), this liberal darling wrote, "I shall never fight in the armed forces with a negro by my side ... Rather I should die a thousand times, and see Old Glory trampled in the dirt never to rise again, than to see this beloved land of ours become degraded by race mongrels, a throwback to the blackest specimen from the wilds." [48]

The Oglala Sioux Chief Crazy Horse monument carved into the Black Hills of South Dakota has got to go for his commission of war crimes.

Jane Fonda's recognitions and business? True liberals should rescind her two Oscars and other awards, boycott her commercial enterprises, and revoke her business licenses for deliberately providing support to the enemy during an active military conflict.

Liberal troopers with too much time on their hands earn extra credit for connecting any term to racism, no matter how tenuously. When there's no actual relationship between words and discrimination, they fabricate one with a rationale that the word "evokes discrimination and disinviting some people from discussions". Only in their hypersensitive paranoia.

For instance, woke liberal race fanatics see only the single definition of the word "master". Yep, you guessed it – it can only refer to the white European male who bought, sold, worked, and beat slaves and violated their women hundreds of years ago. Period, end of discussion. But wait a sec, pal, it certainly *can* refer to such past figures, but it's also a proper title for an expert or highly skilled person, like a master silversmith or carpenter. It also means "main" or "primary" (master plan). Then, as a verb, it is the act of achieving a high degree of proficiency in a subject or skill (mastering calculus or the French horn).

In July, 2020, CNN came out of the woodwork to re-educate the world on such racially oppressive terms as "Master bedroom" (first used in 1926), the PGA's "Masters' Tournament" (the title was adopted in 1939), and the relationship of computer parts or programs said to have a "master-slave" relationship. [49]

Are the liberal cultural police going to ban masters degrees and masterpieces? Of course they'll order mechanics to attend re-education camps if they utter the terms master and slave cylinder -

integral components of brake systems. These absurdities either stoke racial tensions, dilute meaningful discussions of race to the point of alienating most Americans, or drive rational people to simply disregard the topics altogether.

Not to be outdone by CNN, the "Words Matter Task Force" at the University of Michigan's IT Department finds the term "brown bag" racially offensive and substitutes "lunch and learn". The word "picnic" is deemed equally offensive by the UM speech police, even though it originated in Europe in the 1700s. "Abuser" is replaced with "Person who uses drugs", which clearly combines those who abuse drugs with those who take them as prescribed by their physician.[50]

The etymology of other words that no emotionally-stable American associates with racism are included in the growing liberal hallucination: eyelash (because it may evoke images of whip lashings that overseers unleashed on slaves), Peanut Gallery, Godfathered (as used in law), cakewalk, blackball, black mark, angel food cake (lighter color) and devil's food cakes (darker color).

Aunt Jemimah pancake mix, Land-O-Lakes butter (that featured an American Indian in its logo), Uncle Ben's Rice, Elmer Fudd (he carries a shotgun for hunting Bugs Bunny - *certainly* can't have that!) Mrs. Butterworth's syrup, and the Washington Redskins pro football team. They've all gotta go! Are Dixie Cups next?

Are they so narrowly-focused, delicate, and fragile? What bizarre polish do they use on their world-view lenses to construe every action, word, or expression as an offense? And then believe they have a government or university-enforced right to impose such nonsense on others? How do they even have time to think up all of this?

There's really no end to the delirium. Is it now racist for accountants to say that profitability is being "In the black"? Why not require bookkeepers to use blue ink?

Is it also racist to call the first day many businesses achieve profitability each year as "Black Friday"?

Why do liberals tolerate a disproportionate number of black players on NBA and NFL teams? Should we lower the basket height for less-athletic or shorter Whites and Asians to achieve racial balance, like we do with academic standards?

I've Had Enough!

Isn't it grossly unfair to staff college social science departments with predominantly liberal/socialist/communist faculty? Doesn't the government have an obligation to withhold federal funding from those whose proportion of conservatives are less than their representation nationally?

Why does every community have to have a MLK street to avoid charges of racism, and not have to have a Washington, Jefferson, and Adams Street?

Why aren't people who recognize "the first black female Muslim in congress" denounced as racists, sexists, and religious bigots? Why don't people denounce black movies and TV shows that stereotype the appearance and behavior of white people, males in particular?

The mostly self-serving, ever expanding college diversity industry has created entire, highly-paid career fields to address issues that either don't exist or are of marginal consequence (per the Emory example). These issues require much more fundamental actions, or must be resolved by students themselves through life experience and/or counselling for irrational obsessions ("I don't feel valued, respected, or safe", "I pronounce that the college isn't inclusive", or "I'm offended").

Squandering time, attention, and money on frivolous cultural absurdities elevates their contrived relevance. More importantly, that same focus plunders attention and resources from significantly more substantive needs. How does expunging the term "master bedroom" compare to the benefits of changing the victim culture of poverty-stricken inner-city youth?

6. Declare Rampant Police Brutality
Fear-mongering headlines promoting this widely-contrived and extensively hyped political power campaign are a demonstrable lie. Sure, they're some bad departments and cops, and some of those cops have been tried for murder and sentenced to prison. Their miniscule proportion, however, doesn't begin to approach liberals' fanatical claims about police brutality. This topic is reviewed in detail in Chapter 10.

2020 saw a surge of urban criminal mob behavior; Portland, OR surpassed 100 nights of marches, burning, violence, and arson. Several significant conditions there converged into a perfect storm, beginning with decades of liberal government and higher education on how racist and unfair America is. Also, an attitude that anyone who's dissatisfied with their current status or where they're headed is a victim of either "the man" or "the system." Personal and family responsibilities are omitted from all discussions.

Another condition is ignorance of what it takes to lawfully get ahead in our complex society (or choosing not to expend the effort to do so). See Chapter 15 for a detailed discussion. Without that knowledge and the perseverance to implement it, too many failing people vent their frustrations by attacking businesses and other displays by those who've committed to succeed. The overall frustrations of dealing with the COVID virus-related upsets must also be included in aggravating circumstances.

The dysfunction in major cities contributes to additional seething frustration in poorly-served neighborhoods where many inner-city minority members have developed their own "gangsta" culture, one that is painfully aware of their poverty, vilifies education, and glorifies criminal activity. To them, authority, especially the police, becomes the reincarnated overseers and masters of old – deserving enmity and revenge.

The liberal media's incessantly-biased coverage is a major contributor to the pervasive angst. They regularly report incendiary one-sided rumors (the two-year Russian collusion hoax) instead of doing actual journalistic investigation for truth. The media perpetuates a completely false narrative of unrestrained police killings and is a more than willing accomplice in the martyrdom of felons.

This summer also raised the profile of the anarchist Antifa movement. While its name derives from Anti-Fascist, it is demonstrably the epitome of fascism. Like Democrat KKK members of old, today's masked Antifa mobs threaten the public, often hijacking non-violent protests and physically attacking police, businesses, and government buildings with frozen water bottles, bricks, PVC spears, commercial-grade fireworks, and Molotov cocktails. Too many liberal Democratic mayors and city councils either sit idly by, encourage them with bland public pronouncements, or join in. Even then-Democrat presidential candidate Joe Biden wouldn't condemn the Antifa movement during the first 2020 presidential debate.

7. "Mr. Trump, Tear Down This Wall!"

Liberals always accompany this southern border demand with at least one picture of a desperate mother fleeing Central America with her small children, preferably crossing a river or exhausted in the desert. The image tugs at the old heartstrings, right? Liberal strategists encourage the illegal entry of Latin American masses to build their power base with a lure of government largesse; they relentlessly feign sympathy while telling the underclass they're victims of political enemies and never mention any underclass members' personal inadequacies and imperatives to assimilate and improve.

To help maintain a permanent underclass of gullible supporters, liberals embrace groups like Chicago-based Pueblo Sin Fronteras (PSF). Under executive director and left-wing activist Emma Lozano, that group organized and led caravans of thousands of Central Americans towards the U.S. Are they truly refugees, or simply people looking for promised U.S. family-paid benefits?

The United Nations High Commission for Refugees states that a refugee is "someone who is unable or unwilling to return to their country of origin owing to a well-founded fear of being persecuted for reasons of race, religion, nationality, membership of a particular social group, or political opinion." [51]

The UN also indicates support for a principle that European Union countries established in the Dublin Regulation, namely, that refugees fleeing a threat shall seek asylum in the first safe state. Following that principle, people fleeing Central American countries such as Honduras, Guatemala, and El Salvador shall seek asylum in Mexico - the first safe state they enter. Continuing to the U.S. is no longer seeking asylum from homeland oppression, but people shopping for better benefits.

Is America turning its back on legal immigration? Certainly not! The nation's record on immigrant naturalizations has remained rather steady, as shown in these Department of Homeland Security numbers. [52]

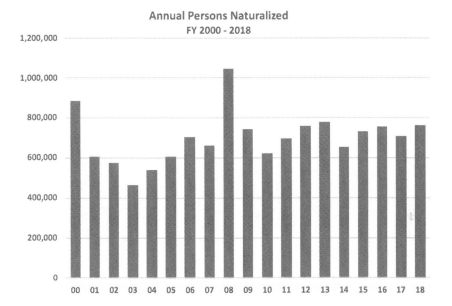

Annual Persons Naturalized
FY 2000 - 2018

For good measure, liberal media and senior elected officials stoke the immigration fires by resurrecting stories about President Trump "putting children in cages". Cages, really? What's going on down there? Do officials actually separate kids from moms? Yes, they do get separated in compliance with rules and in facilities emplaced and followed during the Obama administrations.[53] Now put the emotion aside and take an objective look.

If the police pull you over for drunken driving with your kids in the front seat, would the cop ticket you and send you on your way with the kids? No, of course not. He'd arrest you and place the kids in temporary protective custody. That's what's happening on the border. Immigration officials cannot automatically know if women claiming to be mothers actually are, or if they're using someone else's children to get more favorable consideration. Worse, are they kidnapping children or smuggling the kids to sell as sex slaves? Let's separate them until we answer these serious questions. Real life is much more complicated than the emotional, pixie dust world liberals inhabit.

Do you lock your doors at night? Of course you do. When there's a knock at the door do you confirm who's there before letting them in? Yes again. It's not because you hate everyone outside, it's because you love everyone inside. The same precautions and confirmations you take at your house are applicable for our national "house". Is this conservative scare mongering? Hardly. The Department of Homeland Security's Immigration and Customs Enforcement agency removes over a quarter million illegals annually, the preponderance of whom are convicted criminals:

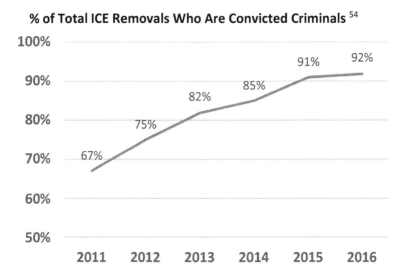

% of Total ICE Removals Who Are Convicted Criminals [54]

Too many liberals parade through their self-designated sanctuary cities to blindly invite anyone through their city's front door, blind to the impact on the community. A more responsible approach in 2019 alone could have prevented more than:[55]
- 1,900 convictions and charges for *homicide*;
- 1,800 convictions and charges for *kidnapping*;
- 45,000 convictions and charges for assault;
- 67,000 convictions and charges for crimes involving drugs;
- 74,000 convictions & charges for Driving Under the Influence.
- Over 12,000 sex offenses, with more than 5,000 convictions and charges for sexual assault;
- Over 10,000 convictions and charges for weapons offenses; and
- More than 74,000 convictions and charges for Driving Under the Influence.

It's vital that we and every other country confirm that would-be immigrants we need and welcome are free of communicable disease, aren't criminals or bent on terrorism, and can contribute to their new society rather than become its burden.

It's also necessary that immigrants understand English and how our government works, both of which better enable them to succeed and avoid devious candidates' claims.

There's no doubt that sanctuary city and state officials will recognize the tremendous human, community, and monetary costs that stack up, but they'll never conclude that their policies were responsible. When faced with the budget realities, we already know what the lament will be, "This isn't just *our* city or state in trouble, it's a *national humanitarian crisis* that demands *federal* dollars." That'll be the excuse for another bailout plan for another failed socialist adventure.

s

8. Cultural Appropriation

This is what most people refer to as assimilation or acculturation – a blending of cultural attributes such as religion, fashion, food, language, symbols, and the arts. Liberals label this as exploitation, like the worst aspects of colonialism. They argue that it's taking unique social qualities out of their original context and doing so without any compensation or proper recognition or attribution. Some also argue that cultural elements taken from their original context and reducing them to fashion wear or toys amounts to desecration. So much for attaining the liberal goal of inclusion.

Others claim that appropriation imposes arbitrary boundaries on the usage of different cultures' characteristics limits artistic expression and promotes division and grievances.

For the record, have you ever heard any complaints about less-developed societies appropriating *western* culture, like their use of cars, trucks, aircraft, and ocean liners? Or their appropriation of developed nations' efficient and intricate financial systems and modern agricultural techniques? Women's high fashion? Complex high-rise buildings, suspension bridges and tunnels? Extensive electrical grids and air conditioning? Medical innovations? Should their innovators be screaming "Foul! Cultural appropriation!"?

9. We'll Tell You What You Need To Know, Trust Us

"If you don't read the newspaper, you are uninformed, if you do read the newspaper you are misinformed."

Mark Twain

Twain's media observation is probably more valid today than when he coined it. Liberal officials grant exclusive access to abetting media that promote the party line, CNN being a darling. When that network hosted a 2016 presidential candidate debate, news contributor and two-time Democrat National Committee (DNC) Chairwoman Donna Brazile leaked debate questions to Democrat candidate Hillary Clinton (which also speaks volumes about Clinton's character).

Normally, hosting party primary debates rotates between major television networks. In 2019, however, the DNC refused their sworn enemy, Fox News, from doing so. "Might ask too many tough questions." Up until 2020, the network had participated in every presidential debate.

Liberal media's coverage of even the most consequential stories found them repeatedly publishing non/poorly-researched events, as exemplified by their two-year drumbeat of the Trump-Russia collusion hoax. Other recent examples were CNN's and The Washington Post's blatantly false and defamatory narratives about Covington Catholic High School student Nicholas Sandmann. Their lead stories excoriated this youngster's calm response to an American Indian beating a drum in his face at a 2019 outdoor event in Washington, D.C.

The liberal media couldn't pass up a chance to fabricate a vilifying story that Sandmann, wearing a red cap with the president's MAGA acronym on it, was taunting, threatening, and blocking Nathan Phillips. The damning reports prompted a series of Sandmann lawsuits against those two media giants and five others. As of this writing, CNN and The Washington Post settled for undisclosed terms.

The New York Times ran a June, 2020 opinion by Senator Tom Cotton (R-AR) encouraging the president to use federal troops to quell rioting sparked by a police shooting in Minneapolis.

Numerous Times journalists criticized the decision to publish the senator's opinion, resulting in editorial page director James Bennett resigning. Apparently, the paper doesn't believe a U.S. senators' views are newsworthy if they don't conform with the paper's own liberal opinions.

A month later at The New York Times, conservative opinion editor Bari Weiss resigned due to senior editors' failure to act against unlawful discrimination by leftist colleagues and a hostile work environment. She published a scathing letter supporting her decision, saying in part, "Stories are chosen and told in a way to satisfy the narrowest of audiences, rather than to allow a curious public to read about the world and then draw their own conclusions."[56]

Weiss was formerly an opinion writer and editor at The Wall Street Journal. Ironically, she'd agreed to join the Times as part of that paper's effort to broaden its ideological range of opinions after having been blindsided by President Trump's election. It never ends.

Without any warnings from the Chinese Communist Party, the worldwide spread of the COVID-19 virus forced school and business closures, economies and jobs to reel, lengthy cancellation of all professional and amateur sports and entertainment, and prohibitions against meetings to observe ones faith. As evidence of the virus began emerging, the President banned flights from China. Liberal Speaker of the House Nancy Pelosi response to the threat was to strut through San Francisco's China Town and criticized his move as xenophobic. The media roundly disparaged the President's precaution and wholeheartedly supported Pelosi.

The left routinely labels conservative opinions as "hate speech" or "offensive speech/images" that their allied social media and search engines can ban under rubric like, "It doesn't conform to our community standards." Adherence to their "community standards" conveniently precludes carrying any stories detrimental to their favorite liberals, too. In late 2020, Facebook and Twitter CEOs were on Congress's radar for deliberately censoring breaking stories of Democrat presidential nominee Joe Biden's actions with Ukraine and China, as well as his son's intermediary roles with interests there. Past propagandists would be proud.

9. White Guilt

The goal of this racial marketing theme is to develop a sense in today's Whites that they harbor sins originating from past slavery. It also promotes the idea that all forms of racism against Blacks is pervasive among everyone with white skin. It goes on to insist that all of todays' Whites are morally, socially, and financially obliged to atone with outlandishly-high cash payments and by supporting any inadequately qualified Blacks for college admissions, promotions, and elections. This will be explored more fully in Chapter 7: Reckoning. Many people believe the strategy was quite effective in twice electing Barack Obama to the presidency.

With so many liberal mantras revolve around racism borne of past slavery, it's useful to briefly review that topic in the next chapter.

Chapter 5: Slavery

"Slavery is founded on the selfishness of man's nature – opposition to it on his love of justice."

Abraham Lincoln

S lavery is always a cruel, inhuman, amoral practice that the New York Times Magazine would have you believe white European settlers started here in 1619. Progressives constantly bombard the airwaves, internet, classrooms, and newspapers with unbridled, inflammatory messaging that the entire current American black population is constrained by a 156-year-old slave past it can never fully emerge from Citing Reagan again, "It isn't so much that liberals are ignorant. It's just that they know so many things that aren't so."

Human enslavement, of course, had existed for millennia, with victors forcing the vanquished to perform menial and arduous work without choice or compensation. Enslavements resulted from war, religious differences, even debt, and have infected every race and continent. The Code of Hammurabi in the 18th century BC detailed rewards and penalties for surgeons who operated on free men or slaves.

African tribes sustained their cultures by enslaving each other for centuries before Europeans and Arabs approached their leaders with trade offers. When the British came to Africa for slaves, the Ashanti tribesmen in current day Ghana were leading dealers in human trafficking.

Sidenote: A number of U.S. Blacks wear a kente cloth draped around their necks and shoulders at graduations and other special occasions. This past summer, Speaker of the House Nancy Pelosi and other ranking Democrats garbed in kente cloths concocted a photo-op in an effort to appear supportive of black voters during an election year.

Were they aware the kente cloth was a power symbol of upper-class Ashanti – the principle organizers and beneficiaries of the slave trade?

Tribes were also selective about which slaves they kept and which they traded,

"African slave owners demanded primarily women and children for labour and lineage incorporation and tended to kill males because they were troublesome and likely to flee. The transatlantic trade, on the other hand, demanded primarily adult males for labour and thus saved from certain death many adult males who otherwise would have been slaughtered outright by their African captors."[57]

Russian expansion ended mass enslavement from the Caucasus, so slave raids in Africa proliferated around the time of the Ottoman Empire. Between the 7th century and 1920, Arab trans-Saharan and Indian Ocean slave-trading routes saw an estimated 17 million slaves - 40x as many as disembarked in North America.

In present day New Mexico, the Pueblo Indians revolted against their Spanish overlords in 1680, masters who'd imposed Catholicism on them, suppressed their culture, and used them as forced labor.

Slave Voyages: The Transatlantic Slave Trade Database is an exhaustive on-going study of 36,000+ trans-Atlantic slave trading voyages. This gold-standard of information estimates 12,521,337 slaves were embarked on slave ships from Africa to the New World from 1501 to 1875. Of those, 3.1%, or 388,746, arrived in mainland North America.[58] Another 52,403 slaves disembarked in North America from intra-American countries, bringing the North American total to 441,149 – 3.5% of the total Africans embarked from Africa for the New World.[59] The remaining 96.5% landed in Brazil, Barbados, Jamaica, Cuba, Mexico, and other countries or were lost during the passage.

Slave disembarkations in North America reached a peak during the period 1751-1775 with 139,959 and declined precipitously afterwards. Slavery also impacted how the Founders crafted the emerging federal Constitution. Some uninformed or agenda-driven critics opine that even that cornerstone document is racist because it counted "other Persons", i.e. Blacks, as only 3/5 of a person.[60] Southern delegates at the 1787 Constitutional Convention argued that slaves should count as a whole person. Doing so, of course, would authorize them more Representatives in the House to block anti-slavery legislation.

Northern delegates vociferously responded that anyone counting towards a state's number of Representatives must enjoy the full rights and privileges of citizenship, which slaves certainly did not. Convention delegates ultimately settled on the 3/5 rule, whereby each slave only counted that lesser number towards representatives in the House. Today's leftist ideologues fail to recognize such a necessary compromise to even *bring about* a United States. With an eye to ultimately achieving full equality, the approved Constitution also prohibited the importation of slaves after 1808.[61]

Black historian Carter G. Woodson (Harvard PhD, 1912) used the 1830 census to compile an exhaustive enumeration of free Blacks and how many slaves they owned. Thomas Pressly's subsequent analysis of that work shows just under 14% of free Blacks owned almost 13,000 slaves in 1830. The Choctaw, Cherokee, Creeks, and Chickasaw tribes west of Arkansas collectively held 7,369 black slaves.[62]

Slaves worked on southern plantations as well as the middle colonies and into New England, and did so longer before 1800 than afterwards.[63] Owners worked slaves in a range of tasks, from field work and household staff to trades. In their efforts to be self-sufficient, 18th century Chesapeake planters and others in the south trained slaves to perform a variety of skilled jobs: carpentry, masonry, boatman, seamstress, blacksmithing, dockhand, and in factories.

Slave housing was bare bones: log, board or brick walls and, more often than not, a shake roof. An open fireplace provided heat for warmth and cooking. Absent effective insulation, they could be cold in winter and insufferably miserable in hot, humid summers.

Some work was organized into unskilled "gangs" that collectively labored at set tasks from dawn to dusk under the eyes of overseers and black drivers who ensured productivity through the lash. Field work was especially repetitive and mind-numbing. The development of cotton farming required very large numbers of gang laborers in fields from the east coast to Texas, bent over the crop in the stereotypical image we associate with slave labor.

Planting, tending, and harvesting rice was done on a task basis; when completed, those slaves had personal time to hunt, fish, or work for their families.[64] Sometimes the pace was seven days a week, while other masters granted a day off a week or month. Punishments included whipping, castration, mutilation, killing, and discounted sales to less humane owners.

Slave diets may consist of pork, some beef, wild game, oysters, fish, nuts and berries, cornbread, an occasional sweet potato, and sometimes milk. Booker T. Washington describes his mother waking him and his siblings to eat chicken that she'd taken from the plantation.

What impact did such diets, oppressive labor, and rudimentary health care have on generations of slaves' pre- and post-natal development and condition? At the 1906 11th Conference for the Study of Negro Problems, American historian, sociologist, author, and civil rights activist W.E.B. Du Bois' presented *The Health and Physique of the Negro American* to attending scholars, health care professionals, and activists. They resolved that the Conference "does not find any adequate scientific warrant for the assumption that the Negro race is inferior to other races in physical build or vitality."[65]

Slavery's remaining days in America *were* numbered, however. Rhode Island enacted an emancipation law in 1775, and half of the original states had abolished the practice within 24 years after the Declaration of Independence.

While a number of European countries participated in the slave trade and their government officials condoned or ignored slavery, efforts eventually took hold to end the practice overseas. Revolutionary France abolished slavery in 1794; in 1807 the British parliament abolished such trading, although it took another 26 years to force emancipation of slaves in British colonies.

As descendants of primitive hunters who immigrated from Asia, the Nermernuh people migrated south and east from Wyoming. They evolved into the Comanche tribe and more effectively adapted to horsemanship than any other warrior in the world. Thus empowered, they thoroughly dominated the Great Plains; every other tribe and many European settlers and soldiers fell before them, were enslaved, or traded. When trading their captives to other tribes, children were routinely separated from mothers, never to be reunited.

How did Indian slaves' treatment compare to that of slaves? Surviving white mother Rachel Parker Plummer, pregnant when captured, then starved and beaten, described how the Comanches dealt with her seven-week-old baby. Her master saw the child as a distraction from her duties of skinning buffalo hides, whereupon she was held while other warriors strangled the baby, then handed him to her. When the infant showed signs of life, the men tied a rope about the baby's neck and dragged him behind a horse through cactus, then around a 100-yard course. He was both dead and torn to pieces.[66] The Tonkawa plains tribe in Texas was known for its cannibalism. Such were realities in North America. Emory University sophomore Peraza and President Wagner would not have fared well on the Great Plains.

No, early colonial America certainly wasn't the first country to see slavery, nor was it even the dominant country in the Americas to accept slaves. The issue was coming to a head, though. In 1857, all seven Democrat Justices on the Supreme Court ruled that the U.S. Constitution wasn't meant to include American citizenship for black people, whether they were free or slaves.[67] The two Republican justices dissented and one, Benjamin R. Curtis, resigned on principle – the only Supreme Court Justice ever to do so. The majority ruling, decried as the worst in the high court's history, also increased tensions between slave-holding states and free-states.

Following the secession of eleven slave-holding states, southern forces initiated the Civil War in 1861.[68] It proved to be our deadliest ever, with an estimated 620,000 deaths (WWII comes in a distant second with 405,000 deaths).[69]

The United States signed an anti-slavery treaty with Great Britain in 1862 allowing their respective navies to intercept each other's flagged ships that were carrying slaves, important to the U.S. because Britain had a much larger navy to perform that duty. That same year President Lincoln issued the Emancipation Proclamation to formally free slaves, though it would take the Civil War to enforce it.

As recounted earlier, not all slaves have been Africans or even Blacks. For every individual slave, however, bondage was abhorrent, and inquisitive readers will wonder how the U.S. slave experience compared with the scope and brutality of other widespread abuses. Many and much more recent examples of mass oppression not only rivaled American slaves' experience, but in many cases significantly exceeded the cruelty of American masters (who at least had a very real economic incentive to keep their slaves fit enough to work).

In 1940s Europe, millions of ordinary men and women were forced to labor for Germany's socialist Third Reich while that regime also experimented on, severely oppressed, tortured, and tormented other millions in concentration camps. Four and a half *million* Jews were simply murdered by starvation, firing squads and in gas chambers. Nazis kept their gold teeth fillings, cut their hair for use as insulation and other products, then burned their corpses. Millions more Russian prisoners on Germany's Eastern Front were worked to death or simply left to die from starvation and the frigid, wind-swept winter.

In July 22, 1942 S.S. Brigadefuehrer Juergen Stroop famously reported that the Warsaw Ghetto Jews were not dying fast enough, so Nazis moved 310,000 of them to extermination camps and gassed them to death. The remaining 60,000 were attacked with tanks, flamethrowers, and artillery.

In October of the same year, SS firing squads killed 16,200 residents of Minsk in a day. By March, 1943 the four groups of death squads had massacred 633,300 Jews in Russia – a full 50% more people than all the slaves brought to North America over a period of 200 years.[70]

Some historians consider the estimate low of 18 million forced labor inmates of the Soviet Union's labor camps between 1930 and 1953 - 42x the number of slaves brought to North America.

Up to 45 million Chinese died from 1958-1962 during Mao Tse-tung's attempts to build his vision of a socialist Eden, yet many leftists today revere him as a role model as their preferred form of government. That's 115x the number of slaves brought to North America.

More recently, Cambodian communist Pol Pot was responsible for the death of up to two million of his countrymen between 1975 – 1979; 4.7x the number of slaves brought to our continent over a hundred years earlier.

With no intent to dismiss or make light of American slaves' treatment and conditions, these and a litany of other cases demonstrate the relative magnitude and depths of man's inhumanity towards all races and nationalities. How has America moved forward since formally abolishing slavery?

I've Had Enough!

Chapter 6: Towards A More Perfect Union

As northern armies marched farther and farther south and victory was more assured, the question arose, "What to do with the Negroes?" Of the estimated 14 million people living in the slave-holding states when the war ended, four million of those Southern souls suddenly and without preparation confronted the most fundamental changes of their lives, changes most could not begin to comprehend; from having a master and overseer directing every facet of their lives to feeling the burden of all those responsibilities suddenly weighing on their own shoulders.

Seven months after the war ended, states ratified the 13th Amendment to the U.S. Constitution, declaring that "Neither slavery nor involuntary servitude, except as a punishment for crime whereof the party shall have been duly convicted, shall exist within the United States, or any place subject to their jurisdiction."

Consider that the vast majority of these freed men and women, nearly one third of those states' combined population, had absolutely no history, culture, development, training, experience nor psychological preparation and adjustment for affairs they were suddenly expected to accomplish. They were abruptly confronted with the necessity of providing their own food, shelter, clothing, acquisition of seed, tools, draft stock, arable land, harvesting and selling their own crops.

They were simultaneously thrust into completely foreign concepts essential to their new lives, concepts most hadn't even been *aware* of before: leases, rents, deeds, debt, interest, sales, taxes, licenses, and contracts. Their inherited slave culture had been one of tardiness, carelessness, neglected work, and subservience. Saving for a mule or old age? Hardly; their concept of the future was the end of the day. Most were unable to read, write, or exercise critical and abstract thinking and judgement. It wasn't that they all lacked the capacity, but their former masters denied them an education to avert rebellions.

W.E.B. Du Bois observed that black slaves had been trained as "… willing and good-natured, but not self-reliant, provident, or careful."[71] It was exceedingly difficult for most of them as freedman, then, to grasp the opportunities so recently opened to them in a society they'd never been assimilated into.

Four months after states ratified the 13th Amendment, Congress enacted the Civil Rights Act of 1866 over the veto of Democrat President Andrew Johnson. The law mandated that "All persons born in the U.S. (except American Indians) were declared to be citizens of the U.S. and granted full and equal benefit of all laws." Unfortunately, it was much too loosely adhered to in the former Confederate states.

Governments were equally unprepared for addressing the monumental needs facing four million people whose care and direction were suddenly reassigned from masters to...whom? The federal government grappled with simply comprehending the magnitude of assimilating so many people into a culture and society that was so vastly different from one they'd lived for ten generations.

The federal government did try, though, through the congressionally-approved U.S. Bureau of Refugees, Freedmen, and Abandoned Lands. Popularly known as the Freedman's Bureau, this office operated courts, established hospitals, and dispensed over 21 million rations during its 7-year existence. It's also remembered for educating Blacks through over 1,000 black schools and creating a number of black colleges and universities – Atlanta University, Fisk University, and Howard University among them. Over fifty civilian relief organizations sent clothes, money, schoolbooks, and teachers southward.[72]

General Sherman's 1865 Field Order #15 designated land from the South Carolina and Georgia coasts 30 miles inland for slaves – 40 acres per family and an army mule. The Bureau was unable to follow through on Sherman's order when President Andrew Johnson nullified it, though, and was forced to simply oversee sharecropping arrangements.

The Republican Congress also incorporated and chartered the Freedman's Savings and Trust Company in 1865 to guide and encourage economic development in black communities. Like the Obama administration's $521 million loss with Solyndra, though, the Freedman's Bank failed. After a mere nine years, bad business deals with depositors' savings led to its demise and generations of Blacks have been wary of financial institutions ever since.

Compounding the physical issues of food, clothing, and shelter were deep-seated emotions ranging from sincere compassion and concern to ambivalence and downright hatred. Suddenly, yesterday's house staff and field hands were now freedmen and Constitutional equals to their traditioned former owners.

Because millions of freedmen constituted a significant number of workers, they were also detested as much, if not more so, for the increased competition they brought to the labor market. That huge labor pool didn't escape the minds of Whites already scratching for work after a devastating war. Nor did the labor pool escape the predatory eyes of immoral landowners, merchants, and other assorted cheats who descended to prey on the newly-freed slaves.

The 14th Amendment, ratified in 1868, affirmed that *all* persons born or naturalized in the U.S. and subject to its jurisdiction are citizens and entitled to equal protection under the law, thus curing the concessionary 3/5 rule discussed in the last chapter. Despite these major legislative accomplishments, Blacks were still heavily discriminated against in the south. Those states responded to the new federal measures by enacting restrictive Black Codes, or "Jim Crow laws" that kept Blacks subservient, segregated, and vulnerable to exploitation as cheap labor.

After the Civil War, glaring inequalities in law enforcement resulted in convict peonage. Southern law enforcement arrested and their courts convicted Blacks of the most insignificant "crimes" and incarcerated them. Whites were then able to cheaply contract with the prison for black "convict" labor: legal post-war slavery.

Blacks, quite naturally, looked upon the whole legal system as racist – a feeling that persists among many of them today. That doubt and skepticism carried over when Blacks were arrested for actual serious crimes, too. Their community refused to believe the sheriff's charges, white witnesses, and white juries' fairness. The deterrent effect of Blacks' own collective opinion about crime was also diminished. Even with video or overwhelming evidence enumerated by black justice officials today, many Blacks are quick to martyr a black criminal who's resisting arrest with lethal force and is subsequently killed by the police.

I've Had Enough!

Reconstruction and assimilation weren't the only issues facing a healing nation whose president had been assassinated less than a month after the Civil War ended. The federal government purchased Alaska from Russia, President Andrew Johnson was impeached, and murderous Indian wars raged in the Great Plains. By 1869 Americans spanned the continent by rail and the country narrowly avoided a national depression following the Black Friday gold scandal.

The following decade, the 15th Amendment specifically prohibited governments from denying citizens the right to vote and Hiram Revels became the first Black sworn into the U.S. Congress. The population increased over 22% from the decade before, and Germany's Kaiser Wilhelm I arbitrated an international boundary dispute between America and Great Britain. An 1873 depression stretched out for five years and the Indian Wars dragged on in the west. President Teddy Roosevelt ordered construction of the Panama Canal and lawyer Charles Guiteau assassinated Roosevelt's successor, James A. Garfield.

In 1889 President Harrison opened up Oklahoma to 50,000 settlers who waited at the starting line for their 160-acre parcel of land. [73] Yes, the country had a lot on its plate through 1890, but not enough of its business helped assimilate Blacks through education, jobs, and building their own wealth. Even though gains were made, Du Bois argued that the country still "failed the Negro" in participating in America's ideals in three significant ways.

First, by denying Blacks the right to vote (Southern states had enacted poll taxes and literacy tests to blunt the 15th Amendment). Second, by forcing Blacks into a lower caste: merchants were indebted to wholesalers, planters to merchants, tenants to planters, and laborers at the bottom; of course, a number of Whites lived in poverty also.[74] Southern Whites enforced such discrimination through "legal" measures and social obstacles: a profusion of the Jim Crow laws mandated segregation in public facilities. Du Bois' third enumerated failure was denying Blacks the higher education that the capable among them were qualified to obtain.[75]

70 years later, the country was in the throes of the Great Depression and thousands of homeowners were on the verge of losing

their homes. Voters elected Franklin D. Roosevelt president in 1933 and as part of his New Deal promise, he created the Home Owners' Loan Corporation (HOLC). That office purchased mortgages from banks and amortized them over a much longer period and at lower interest rates than banks did. As a result, owners who sold their home before paying off the mortgage were now able to keep the accumulated equity.

To avoid its own default, the HOLC used local private real estate agents to assess loan risks for individual homes as well as surrounding neighborhoods. Back then, racially-mixed neighborhoods were considered less stable and, therefore, more financially risky. The National Association of Real Estate Boards' manual went so far as to warn member agents against introducing races into a neighborhood that would be detrimental to its property values. [76]

The resulting HOLC product was a series of color-coded maps, with neighborhoods deemed the least financially risky shaded in green and the riskiest in red. Even if Blacks lived in a stable middle-class neighborhood, it was colored red simply due to the assessed financial risk the agents associated with its racial composition. The HOLC did rescue some homeowners in red zones, but it was now clearly incorporating race into key housing policies.

In 1934, Congress and President Roosevelt formed the Federal Housing Administration (FHA) to insure 80% of a new buyer's home price. With that guarantee, banks were much more willing to lend money to new home-buyers. The problem? The FHA wouldn't insure home loans in neighborhoods of mixed-races or that were near black neighborhoods where integration may occur later. In other words, black Americans need not apply.

In response to the millions of servicemen returning from WWII, the Veterans Administration (VA) began guaranteeing their mortgages. However, devious southern Democrats blunted GI Bill of Rights provisions for returning black veterans. House Veterans Committee Chairman John Rankin (D-MS) insisted the Bill be administered at the state level, giving southern states authority to implement rules that effectively denied benefits to Blacks.[77] He sought to prevent injured black veterans from treatment in Veterans Administration hospitals, underfunded black colleges, reduce death payments to certain black veterans by 40%, supported poll taxes, and blocked a federal anti-lynching bill.

When the Federal Housing Administration later spurred construction of massive (17,000 unit) residential developments, it and the VA made builders promise not to sell new homes to Blacks. The practice had several consequences, none of them in keeping with our national ideals.

Denied the expansive housing market prompted by the federal government, a number of Blacks were limited to existing inner-city ghettos of rental units. This also restricted their ability to build home equity, as their white peers were doing in government-underwritten developments like Levittown. A lack of home-loan funding also stunted development in minority zones, which contributed to segregation in many cities for generations.

As late as 1951, Birmingham, AL enforced its Racial Segregation Ordinance that included these provisions:

<u>SECTION 369. SEPARATION OF RACES</u>. It shall be unlawful to conduct a restaurant or other place for the serving of food in the city, at which white and colored people are served in the same room, unless such white and colored persons are effectually separated by a solid partition extending from the floor upward to a distance of seven feet or higher, and unless a separate entrance from the street is provided for each compartment.

<u>SECTION 1413. SEPARATION OF RACES.</u>
Every owner or operator of any jitney, bus or taxicab in the city shall provide equal but separate accommodations for the white and colored races by dividing separate vehicles or by clearly indicating or designating by visible markers....

<u>SECTION 597. NEGROES AND WHITE PERSONS NOT TO PLAY TOGETHER</u>. It shall be unlawful for a negro and a white person to play together or in company with each other in any game of cards or dice, dominoes or checkers.

SECTION 939. SEPARATION OF RACES.
It shall be unlawful for a negro and a white person to play together or in company with each other at any game of pool or billiards.

In 1963, Alabama's Democrat Governor George Wallace emphatically declared during his inauguration speech, "Segregation now, segregation tomorrow, segregation forever!" In Birmingham, Democrat Commissioner of Public Safety Eugene "Bull" Connor ordered firefighters to turn high-pressure fire hoses on civil rights demonstrators and for police to intimidate black marchers with dogs.

The same year, members of the Ku Klux Klan detonated a bomb at the Black 16th Street Baptist Church in Birmingham, killing four young girls. That atrocity further energized the civil rights movement under Dr. Martin Luther King, who preached and practiced a non-violent approach to the cause. The efforts were a major influence in passage of the 1964 Civil Rights Act and the 1965 Voter Rights Act. Liberals in both chambers of the U.S. Congress who paint themselves as "defenders of the little guy" provided less support than their conservative counterparts for each of these landmark legislative victories:[78]

	House Support		Senate Support	
	Dem.	Rep.	Dem.	Rep.
1964 Civil Rights Act	60%	**76%**	61%	**79%**
1965 Voting Rights Act	75%	**80%**	69%	**94%**
1968 Fair Housing Act	68%	**87%**	66%	**81%**

A century and a half of very different experiences couldn't help but have a different impact on black Americans' outlooks, attitudes, and opinions.

I've Had Enough!

Chapter 7: Perspectives

While some Blacks were able to take advantage of the new opportunities and many others never could or did, they all had something in common: the very distinct history of a race that had borne generations of bondage and injustice. They survived entire lives of discrimination at every turn. A shared history of hardships bound them together ever more tightly, like one family that's psychologically and emotionally aligned in its fight for survival and equality.

In his 1903 book *The Souls of Black Folk,* W.E.B. Du Bois' describes a Veil through which Blacks viewed the world, a view that's different from that of Whites.[79] The Constitution declares that all men are created equal, yet Jim Crow laws and any number of more subtle discriminations rendered them unequal.

As with any very large group of people, Blacks have individual characteristics, beliefs, ideals, and behaviors; they aren't a monolithic race that always thinks alike or moves in one direction at a single speed or intensity. Many (most?) American Blacks' primary identity, however, is with their race, with its shared cruel beginning amidst a sea of white faces.

After a miserable ocean voyage (about 16% of trans-Atlantic slaves died before reaching mainland North America) their senses absorbed a new land of completely foreign topography, smells, flora, fauna, language, food, song, and routines that were unlike any they'd ever encountered. They couldn't read, but even if they could, there were no histories or written records of their heritage *to* read. They acquired what they knew of ancestors and origins through stories and song. They endured lives struggling in fields, shops, kitchens, and factories until finally freed by death.

The idea of a national origin didn't exist. Captured by rival tribesmen at an early age from land they'd hunted or farmed, one wonders if descendants were even fully aware of what village or tribe they'd belonged to? They may ask and answer, "Who, then, am I? I am black. I am one of many others who look like me, are abused like me, and question like I do."

I've Had Enough!

Only much later and after a savage war would Blacks here come to know what a nation is, and later still, that the nation they'd lived in had loudly and proudly professed ideals of life, liberty, no cruel or unusual punishments, and equal protection under the law – written even while they and ancestors as far back as they can remember had no such rights. We are Blacks, they are Whites.

Whites came from much different pasts, with long and storied written histories of their lineage. They were aware of differences among nations, regions, economic status, and professions. Ideals of the Constitution applied to them much more evenly and universally.

Too many of those human and civil rights have only recently come about for Blacks, extending the primacy of racial identity over nationality. They are still fighting for full equality that some Whites have overtly opposed, failed to ardently support, choose to ignore, or simply remain unaware of.

The vast difference of the two pasts' goes a long way to reveal why many Blacks and Whites hold such different views of interactions with the law. This comes into sharp focus with police killings, as in George Floyd's 2020 death while in police custody.

Blacks' reaction may sound something like this, "White cops killed another brother, just like they've been doing since they brought us here in chains. Sure, Floyd may have strayed a few times, but he was a good guy and everyone liked him – just out with some friends when the man got him. They don't care about George, though, they murdered him just because he was one of us. It'd all been different if he was White; maybe he'd have just got some jail time.

"They tell us this country is based on equality, but it never happens when a brother's involved. Some things never change. Whites want to feel good and righteous, to overlook the difference between how *we* live and *their* ideas about the "land of the free and justice for all". But they don't stand up against all of the injustice. I just can't understand it."

Then Blacks and progressives go on put the deceased felon on a pedestal as another martyr in their struggle for equality and dignity. The media salivates to capture the emotion but not all the facts. They run prime time footage that omits any criminal record, non-compliance, or threats against the police. Like clockwork, "if it bleeds, it reads" reporting is followed by riots, destruction (often of blacks' businesses), and more deaths.

As black rap artist Lecrae said in 2020, "[there's a] collective history and a collective culture, and collective sense of what's happening. We don't see a single killing, but a historical narrative of this happening again and again." [80] Many other Blacks expressed similar feelings after Floyd's death in police custody. Black Fortune 500 CEO Ken Frazier (Merck & Co.) similarly summed up the incident, "What the African American community sees in that videotape is that this African American man, who could be me or any other African American man, is being treated as less than human." [81]

But not so fast, Mr. Frazier. First of all, you and most other Blacks don't have a lengthy arrest record that includes an armed home invasion and aggravated robbery with a deadly weapon. You also took full advantage of educational opportunities that started you off on a successful career. Then your moral code and work ethic maximized that start and you've never been apprehended for passing suspected counterfeit currency (which is also a felony). Third, you wouldn't have more than three times the level of fentanyl in your system that could cause a fatal overdose. Finally, if you *were* being arrested, I'm confident you wouldn't escalate the situation by physically resisting multiple officers, but would comply with their instructions and let an attorney argue the case in court. I just can't understand it.

Regrettably, the story plays out numerous more times every year (see Chapters 10 and 11).

Elevating a thug and felon like Ferguson, MO's Michael Brown to martyr status when he repeatedly assaulted a police officer numbs the rest of the public to *actual* police transgressions. It even happens when videos show officers performing their duties as respectfully as one would expect them to, and has the end effect of crying "Wolf". If the goal is realistic reforms, proponents have to present their perspective much more effectively to an audience that doesn't embody the same racial past and groupthink they do.

I've Had Enough!

Identifying with race as "family" leads to gut-level emotions that lump people into competing tribes of Blacks, Whites, Asians, Hispanics, etc. It fails to recognize individual people, and whether or not their actions conform to laws passed by everyone's representatives. It also looks past individual successes – those of every race and gender who've overcome life's hurdles. How many Blacks attribute every negative action they observe, experience, or feel as a racially-motivated indignity, discourtesy, or affront? Sometimes, it's a matter of how you interpret them.

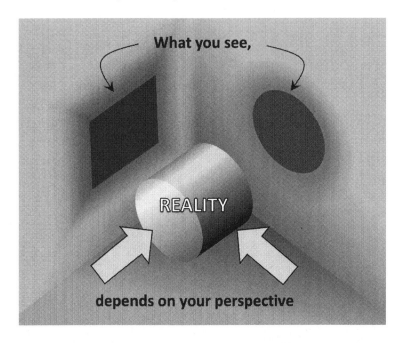

On A Personal Note...

In 1978 I commanded a 25th Infantry Division unit that was due for a major inspection. Two crucial sections needed immediate attention: our field generators and chemical detection equipment. I called on my most technically proficient and motivated NCO, a black sergeant, explained how important the equipment was to our mission, and assigned him the dual mission. He saluted, turned about, and went to work.

Several days later I visited the shops and discovered that even *this* very capable NCO was waging a losing battle – there was just too much to do. I decided the chemical gear was the more important, so I relieved him of any further responsibilities with the generators so he could direct all of his time and talents to the chemical equipment.

Within a day, the battalion Equal Opportunity Officer graced my office door to inform me of a discrimination complaint the SGT lodged against me.

I was dumbstruck; this NCO was top notch and I'd trusted him alone with the outcome of a particularly vital assignment. "What's the complaint?" I asked surprisingly.

"He said you relieved him of an important assignment."

Then it hit me like a proverbial thunderbolt. Due to its very pejorative connotation within the military, "relieve" was the exact wrong word to have used. I'd verbally transmitted a decision to prioritize his talents to the more important task; he heard that I'd just lost complete confidence in him and fired him on the spot. Since I hadn't explained my rationale, he assumed it was racial.

I talked to him later in the day to apologize for my poor word choice, my actual intent, and reiterate my complete confidence in him. We passed the inspection.

This illustrates the very different impressions that two people can draw from a single sentence – one word, actually. Both of us left the brief conversation fully confident of what had just happened. Actually, though, we both got it completely wrong.

I imagine everyone carries some psychological burdens, differing perspectives, and an imperative to act in certain ways, partially from experiences and also from what family and friends pass down. Anyone's particular burden, its intensity, and influence affect their view of the world, their place in it, and how they assess their relevance or significance. Regardless of how intense the burdens, others have risen from more onerous, debilitating depths and with heavier burdens.

Realistically, some level of discrimination will always exist between people who are identifiably-different: males and females, size, age, skin color, and other physical features. Most strive to continually reduce that behavior, but immoral hustlers use the opportune characteristics to divide and conquer. Left-wing politicians employ the strategy all too often with their pervasive identity-politics.

An immediate question then arises, "Beyond life's many encounters and inadvertent interactions, along with people's predispositions, how much *actual* discrimination and disparagement against Blacks is going on now and how much is a matter of perception? There's probably no definitive answer, but I suspect for many Blacks the answer is "too much." How effectively will legislative successes and an ever-growing number of black Representatives, Senators, Mayors, and city council members improve matters?[82]

How much of that discrimination is abated when Blacks hold elected offices? Do they create better, safer havens? More than a third of America's top-100 cities are governed by Blacks, with the vast majority of them Democrats, but that's no assurance they're safe.[83] Chicago, IL is the largest city governed by a Black - Democrat Lori Lightfoot. As of December 27, 2020, the number of murders there increased 55% from the prior year.[84]

Here are the ten cities with populations over 500k that have the highest violent crime rate in 2018[85]:

City	Violent Crime per 100 population	Mayors' Political Party
Detroit	2,008	Dem. since 1962
Memphis	1,943	Dem. since 1982
Baltimore	1833	Dem. since 1967
Milwaukee	1,413	Dem. since 1960
Albuquerque	1,365	1985 except '09-'17
Indianapolis	1,273	Mixed parties
Nashville	1,113	Dem. Since 1963
Houston	1,026	Dem. Since 1982
Chicago	1,006	Dem. since 1931
Washington	941	Dem. since 1961
Philadelphia	909	Dem. since 1982

Those numbers certainly don't demonstrate that Blacks are safer where Blacks and liberals run the government. Why? Too many black politicians, like so many other politicians of every race, seek office for reasons other than public service. Even though liberals talk about solving racial problems, the record above says otherwise .

Despite hurdles that everyone faces, Blacks have reached the summits of the professions. Black entrepreneur Sarah Breedlove (1867–1919) is the earliest documented black female millionaire; she came from the cotton fields. In later life she lived on an estate about three miles from John D. Rockefeller.

President George H. W. Bush selected four-star General Colin Powell as Chairman of the Joint Chiefs of Staff - the senior officer of the world's most capable military. President Bush also chose Condoleezza Rice as U.S. Secretary of State - the senior member of the president's cabinet. The American Express board of directors chose black businessman Ken Chennault to serve as CEO of that Fortune 500 company from 2001 – 2018. Barack Obama served as a two-term President. Those are great, but why haven't *more* Blacks achieved such success?

How do Asians, another visually-distinct minority, do so much better than Blacks? Do they overemphasize a legacy of past injustices, or stress current and future education and lawful behavior? How many Blacks attribute any current real or perceived injustice to a 155-year-old legacy of slavery? Have they self-imposed and culturally-reinforced a self-fulfilling psychosis of victimhood? How have so many other Blacks successfully used opportunities and risen within their communities?

Several years ago a black acquaintance told me, "You just don't get it, *no white person* does." I have more than a passing knowledge of America's slave past, Reconstruction, the Jim Crow era, and residual discrimination. I've lived discrimination as an absolute minority while living in the Caribbean, South Korea, and downtown in Latin America. It's not the same discrimination that today's Blacks experience, of course, but it's racial discrimination none the less. I do *hear* what my black friend told me, but conclude that it isn't a matter of "not getting it." It's that I don't *agree* with his narrative of rampant discrimination, endemic police oppression, rationalizations for perpetual victimization, and failure to achieve more when so many Blacks and other minorities have. He didn't believed I could step into his world and I didn't believe he could step beyond it.

People's strength of character is often gauged by how they deal with adversity. So it was with the Jews' recovery from the murderous era of the Holocaust, where many had been worked to death (in addition to being worked fiendishly hard).

A measure of the Germans' post-WWII character is found in their resurgence as Europe's strongest economy from the ashes of 1,000-plane bomber missions over their cities and decimation of so many of their youth. Similarly the Japanese have rebuilt from intensive homeland bombings that included two atomic bombs.

Many Blacks, other minorities, and yes, the American majority, have also demonstrated similar strengths of character as they live with lingering injustices. Discrimination has diminished significantly from earlier days, but it hasn't been eradicated (and, realistically, never will be). Politicians, race peddlers, and revisionist historians are all too happy to spotlight or invent racial issues and promote division to get elected, gain relevance as a champion, or simply book another paid appearance. They compete to elevate their followers to the title of "most-discriminated against" to obtain special considerations – some justified and some just greedy ambitions.

A paradox of the American identity is its composition of people with many different traditions, motives, and ideals, who possess distinctive qualities that define an American character. Is race or ethnicity that defining characteristic? Or is it the love of liberty, the pursuit of justice, an urge to invent, overcome, and achieve, the drive to explore, the pursuit of individuals' ideas and spiritual values? I think the latter.

Only those who carry psychological burdens can decide how long they will do so, how it will affect them, what they pass on to their children, and whether it will it turn them against other Americans and handicap their future… or not.

"Whether you think you can or think you can't, you're right"

Henry Ford, Industrialist

Chapter 8: Reckoning

"We do not live in the past, but the past in us."

unknown

Modern activists identify three major oppressions against Blacks, beginning well before the Emancipation Proclamation.

First. Frequent voices submit that slaves weren't paid for their labor that built the wealth of America on cotton and other crops; they were undeniably robbed.

We can only acknowledge that owners plundered slaves of their labor under threats of death or great bodily harm. To maximize benefit of the theft, masters often worked their slaves under inhuman conditions, broke families apart, and traded slaves when it was economically advantageous to do so. Benefits accrued directly to the plantation owner, of course, but also to his family, cotton ginners, transporters, textile manufacturers, merchants, and end consumers. To be sure, some slave-holders, especially those with large plantations, became very wealthy.

When cotton was king, the U.S. supplied about 60% of the world's demand, with Whites and freedmen producing as much as slaves. Advances like elective crop breeding and the cotton gin drove increased production that made cotton king.[86] Even then, however, southern crops tilled and harvested by slaves were not the main engine of national prosperity.

That engine, Diedre McCloskey convincingly argues, was ingenuity and innovation, not exploitation by slave-owning southerners. A major engine of that innovation was the land-grant university system that President Lincoln authorized to help the country adapt to the industrial revolution.[87] Consider this sampling of technological firsts from 1801 – 1860: the suspension bridge, flanged T-rails (that are still used on today's railways), the combine harvester, steam shovel, milling machine, lathes, vapor-compression refrigeration, lock-stitch sewing machines, circuit breakers, vulcanized rubber, the rotary printing press, jackhammer, equatorial sextant, escalator, repeating rifle, and the hand-cranked machine gun.

Second. Racial activists readily concede that neither original plaintiffs nor defendants are alive to argue and respond to the well-documented charges of slavery. They now argue that slaves' were prohibited from building any wealth to pass on to their children. Coupled with intervening generations of continued discriminatory practices that obstructed wealth-building (such as home loans and housing restrictions covered in Chapter 5), today's descendants have been cheated. Now they want their unfulfilled inheritances.

Finally, activists cite psychological burdens and emotional indignity that Blacks constantly endure for [real and perceived] treatment as second-class citizens in their own country. They cite the effects of compounded discrimination on other quality of life issues such as education, employment, safety, and health.

The Tuskegee Syphilis Study, conducted by the U.S. Public Health Service, is an outcome of that discrimination. PHS staff injected 600 black sharecroppers with the scourge and followed its effects from 1932 to 1972. Even after a team at the U.S. Marine Hospital Staten Island found penicillin an effective cure in 1943, the USPHS did not use it with the subjects. There's no excuse or defense for such government conduct, which President Clinton recognized in 1997 with a formally apology,

> "… It was a time when our nation failed to live up to its ideals, when our nation broke the trust with our people that is the very foundation of our democracy. It is not only in remembering that shameful past that we can make amends and repair our nation, but it is in remembering that past that we can build a better present and a better future. … Our government is supposed to protect the rights of its citizens; their rights were trampled upon."

The aggrieved and sympathetic supporters hold white individuals, groups, businesses, and governments responsible for failures to recognize and correct still-existing inequities; in short, to bring the American dream of equality to every citizen.

Your value doesn't decrease based on the of inability of others to see your worth.

To those familiar with the exasperation, frustration, and hopelessness, doing nothing in the face of racism becomes a sin of omission; "Get under your neighbor's burden!" they urge. Blacks see that many white Americans are quite conscious of the debt they owe uniformed servicemembers who fought to establish and preserve our liberties from Valley Forge through Normandy, Korea, Viet Nam, and Iraq to Afghanistan. Then they ask, "Why aren't white Americans more conscious, sympathetic, and willing to actively support Blacks who *continue* to bear burdens of inequality? How can you continue to enjoy so much of the Dream with the inequity that's all around you?"

They also posit further questions they associate with oppressions, "Why aren't Blacks admitted to colleges in proportion to their population? Why are Blacks imprisoned in such disproportionate numbers? Why do police proportionately kill so many more Blacks than Whites?" Conspicuously, they never mention that Asians fare so much more favorably in all three areas.

Why indeed do so many inequities exist with Blacks? Not all of them do. Characterizing all police killings of Blacks as modern oppression, lynching, or murder is a blatant lie - a headline to grab the attention of zealous activists, sycophants, and the ignorant. The truth is detailed in Chapter 10.

Even with that reality, why don't more Whites become active in Black causes? Sadly, many Americans today don't even know who the original colonies fought in the Revolutionary War to win our independence, or which nations composed the Axis powers of WWII. Is it any wonder that they are oblivious to issues that most directly affect only 13% of the national population?

When they *do* hear charges of black inequality, they reflect on the litany of major achievements to address them: The Emancipation Proclamation, the Civil War, three Constitutional amendments, federal civil and voter rights legislation of 1866, 1964

93

and 1965, and President Lyndon Johnson's multi *trillion*-dollar Great Society programs. They may also be aware of the 1968 Civil Rights Act and its included Fair Housing Act and the Housing and Urban Development Act of 1968 that expanded home ownership funding. Add in the repeal of discriminatory Jim Crow laws.

Many Asians and Whites endure direct, personal acts of discrimination *themselves* when colleges deduct points on their children's college entrance exams and add them to less academically prepared minority applicants. At work, some also observe companies regularly hiring very minimally-qualified minorities over much more qualified candidates to beef up their racial statistics.

Then they ask, "Tell me again why I need to be on the front lines of those issues instead of dealing with so many of my *own*?"

Just like minority families, these people are fully engaged with priorities of jobs, raising kids, their health, faith, retirement planning, caring for parents or relatives, and almost limitless other demands of life. Will my health insurance cover the cancer the oncologist just diagnosed? Is my soldier son/daughter safe in Afghanistan tonight? How real are the resurgent national threats from China, Russia, North Korea, and Iran? Is my job safe from a downturn? What about the virus from China?

If they're male, family courts may discriminate against them on matters of child custody and alimony. On top of all these challenges, someone is constantly screaming, "You're privileged; you didn't work, make any sacrifices, or take risks for what you've got." Then comes the ultimate but hollow epithet (again and again), "You're a racist!"

Absent more individual activism, are Blacks confident the government will play a larger role? While Americans view government warily, I saw much greater skepticism among the population in Panama while living there in the mid 1980s.

In 1985 the brutally tortured body of Hugo Spadafora was discovered in a mail bag; his slowly-decapitated head never was recovered. Spadafora was an outspoken critic of General Manuel Noriega, the de facto Panamanian national leader and a profiteer from drug and arms deals. Soon after President Barletta promised justice for Spadafora, the general forced Barletta's resignation and worked closely with replacement Eric Delvalle until he had the legislature oust Delvalle two years later. So much for trusting the Panamanian government.

Given that corruption, most Panamanians believed in only two institutions: the family and the church. Readings, observations, and experience suggest that many Blacks here are similarly distrustful of government and harbor a self-fulfilling and self-limiting burden that's prevalent in their culture.

From a personal perspective...

While the basis of self-doubts and fears of discrimination were much less serious than that of Blacks, I recall a situation that was similar in principle during my assignment as aide-de-camp to the post's commanding general. At a formal social occasion, I arrived early to conduct protocol checks and my new bride walked in later as the function was getting underway.

She later recounted her trepidation, a haunting anxiety, almost despair as she walked into the large room filled with officers much more senior than I was. "They're all looking at me! Am I dressed appropriately? They must have much more formal education - what if they ask where I went to college? Will I commit some unrealized social faux pas that reflects poorly on Bob? How can I converse with senior officers and even worse, their wives?"

Of course, all the other attendees *weren't* looking at her; she did great, and none of the feared social catastrophes ensued. She faced her personal doubts and fears and during an assignment years later, effortlessly hosted a dinner party for our two-star commanding general (who the president would later appoint as Chairman of the Joint Chiefs of Staff. Joye and his wife remain in touch).

Many Blacks doubt their standing and potential on much more serious considerations, concerns, and fears. Some of those concerns are well-founded, but how often do they *interpret* tones, looks, words, and actions as demeaning reinforcements of their views? How many perceived slights are the realistic bumps and grinds of actual life, an unintentional snub of everyday social interaction? Are they worth the emotional drain? How do they compare with other threats, like the Chinese Communists' burgeoning military capability and territorial claims and flareups with India?

In an Atlanta Passion City Church roundtable, Pastor Louie Giglio and Chick-fil-A CEO Dan Cathy listened to black hip-hop musician Lecrae discuss what it was like living black. In one example, he responded, "…as soon as I drive into a Wyoming grocery store looking for some products for my hair, they're not going to be there, and once again I'm reminded, oh, I'm black and these products do not exist for me." Was that overt racism, unconscious bias, or was it a straightforward business decision to use limited shelf space for products that the other 98.7% of Wyoming's non-black population was much more likely to purchase?[88]

Whether it's my wife at a high-profile social setting or Blacks in the everyday course of their lives, the impact of self-doubt is personally detrimental, demoralizing, and destructive. So the question arises, how much of current Blacks' "lives behind the Veil" is currently attributable to hardcore discrimination and how much do they interpret as such?

Is W.E.B. Du Bois' 'color line" universal among all races, not only between Blacks and Whites, but also between Whites and Asians?[89] If so, how have Asians assimilated more thoroughly into America's culture and achieved higher scholastic standings, lower crime rates, and median family incomes over 30% higher than Whites and twice that of Blacks? Do Du Bois' color lines exist between Blacks and other races?

I too have some sense of constant personal assaults… by liberals who want to seize the fruit of my labor, direct my grandchildren's education, burden me with their liberty-thieving government dictates, and change the culture for political ends, all without any historical or current evidence that their changes benefit the country and its population.

Does race dominate your identity and outlook? Is it more beneficial or detrimental to place that identity and "not giving up your blackness" above all other personal characteristics, attributes, and traits? Does race always supersede major challenges you've overcome and what you've made of yourself, such as, "born into poverty and became the family's first college graduate?"

A friend of mine had to quit school in the 10th grade to work the family farm, then joined the Air Force when his older brother took over those duties. As soon as he completed his military obligation, he worked as an insurance salesman, then sold cosmetics. Without higher education, but highly motivated, the global cosmetics company promoted him to district, then regional manager, and finally named him national sales manager. He went on to buy a small 7-employee business that he expanded to 150 and knew every one of them by name.

Dissatisfied with county government, he ran for the county commission and was elected its chairman. Political opponents branded him as the most despised man in the county. He qualified as a private pilot in his 50s and flew his own twin-engine Beech Baron until a mild stroke grounded him in his early 80s. Don't any *one* of those accomplishments say more about his character and who he is as a person than simply identifying as a white man?

All of these actual or perceived oppressions have raised the question of reparations – the subject of the next chapter.

I've Had Enough!

Chapter 9: Reparations

Evaluating history without context would doom every nation in the world to living with perpetual guilt for the actions of ancestors behaving consistent with the time.

Kathleen Brush, PhD, CEO, Author

Questions of reparations for *anyone*, of course, raise questions of reparations for *every* person who stakes a claim of direct or indirect injustice.

Reparations for Blacks currently occupy center stage in the discussions, so those voices are loudest and most frequently heard. That, however, doesn't override a broader, national discussion of key questions. Definitions, standards, and procedures have to apply equally to all 330 millions of us and accommodate our considerable diversity; they cannot be crafted just for the most outspoken petitioner of the day. The matter raises three fundamental questions.

#1. Who Are the Oppressed and Aggrieved?

A response to this question becomes very involved very quickly. If freedmen's modern-day descendants receive benefits for enslaved ancestors, shouldn't they also bear some responsibility for compensating descendants of the 360,000 Union soldiers who died to secure their freedom?

Where do American Indians fit into a reparations formula? The government treated them more reprehensibly than freedmen. Nomadic Plains Indians, for example, had hunted immense expanses of America's mid-section for generations until Washington D.C.'s blue-jacketed enforcers confined them into ever smaller hunting grounds and finally onto defined reservations. When west-bound settlers demanded even more, the 1900 Dawes Act granted each Comanche 160 acres, an additional 480,000 tribal acres, and reverted the remainder of their 2 million-acre reservation to federal land for a dollar an acre. Apaches, Arapahos, Kiowas, and others were treated similarly.

In the last major confrontation against Plains Indians, the U.S. Cavalry killed 146 Sioux on the Pine Ridge reservation in

South Dakota in 1890. The federal government confined thousands of Indians of a dozen tribes to reservations where many still live.

What other races or groups have been oppressed and aggrieved? Early Chinese immigrants certainly were. A mob of 500 Whites and Hispanics lynched 17-20 Chinese workers in 1871 in Los Angeles over a dispute. Eight men were convicted but the verdicts were thrown out on a technicality.[90] In 1885 Rock Springs, WY, white miners killed 28 Chinese co-workers, wounded another 15, and drove several hundred others out of town.[91] So, should the plights of Chinese in America and their descendents' oppressions also be considered? Are they on par with, or ahead of, those raised by Blacks?

Racist attitudes against Italian immigrants were the basis of the 1891 mob that lynched 11 Italians in New Orleans. Quick-mouthed liberal politicians and media, like today's, fanned the flames surrounding the assassination of the city's police chief by declaring Italian suspects guilty of murder before they ever went to trial. *The New York Times* called the Italian victims "desperate ruffians and murderers. These sneaking and cowardly Sicilians, the descendants of bandits and assassins... are to us a pest without mitigations."[92]

Added to such grievances are those of our major ethnicity, Hispanics, and there are 44% more of them than Blacks.[93] The federal 1946 Mendez, et. al. v Westminister case challenged segregation against Mexicans in Orange County, CA schools and resulted in the repeal of many segregationist provisions in that state's laws. The landmark 1954 U.S. Supreme Court case of Hernandez v. Texas established 14th Amendment protection from Jim Crow laws for Hispanics, Asians, Middle Easterners, Inuit, Native American, and other non-Whites and Blacks.[94]

Should we, or *can* we, include descendants of those who labored amid numerous injustices to build the foundations for our current life of freedom and largesse? Laborers and tradesmen who constructed railroads, canals, roads, bridges, and tunnels, as well as adults and children who toiled in hazardous factories. Soldiers and sailors who died or were maimed fighting the Kaiser, the Führer and Emperor of Japan?

R.J. Ross

The Okies eking out a bare existence during the dust bowl years in Oklahoma also faced injustices while building our modern life; should their descendants join the pool of today's Blacks insisting on reparations?

What, then, is a fair and proper standard for deciding who should qualify for reparations?

Racial mouthpiece Al Sharpton lobbies to examine who was "adversely impacted by the peculiar institution [of slavery]"[95]. Is it practical, even possible, to prove who they are? Rashawn Ray and Andre M. Perry at the Brookings Institution argue that every Black who can show they were excluded from various policies since the Emancipation are eligible for damages. What shall constitute proof they were excluded?

Ray's and Perry's standard translates into *every* Black in the country, even those who immigrated within the past decades – long after the imposition of major Constitutional amendments; enactment of civil, voting, and housing rights; equitable mortgage loans; college admissions preferences, etc. Is that a proper standard? If so, it would include millionaire Senator Corey Booker, multi-millionaires Barack and Michelle Obama, and their daughters. Does it make sense to include so many people who've already risen beyond past oppressions through the education, jobs, and entrepreneurial opportunities they've maximized?

A fair consideration of who merits redress, then, may easily include a majority of the present population. An additional complication is that many of their ancestors were also oppressors, like American Indians forced onto reservations and who'd also owned slaves. Do their ancestors' oppressions offset each other? How should we treat Blacks who owned slaves? [96]

The baseline in our society to determine victimization has been and should remain the laws in effect at *the time of an alleged violation*. Plaintiffs who believe they have sufficient evidence to prove an allegation must petition the courts.

However we answer the question of inclusion, there'll be an immediate, clamoring swarm of others to climb aboard the train.

#2. Who Shall Be Held Accountable?

The standard for accountability must be whether the alleged violator has unlawfully wronged another - has a law been broken or a contract gone unfulfilled?

There's a tendency to think only in terms of today's norms and laws. We're generally ignorant of and shrink from knowing the culture and society of the past. Therefore, we're quick to employ presentism - applying today's standards, to judge past people and institutions. But we have to remain true to the laws of the land at the time they were in effect to determine whether a party has committed a violation and the extent to which it may be compensable.

A proper starting point is asking "What legal agreements were in effect between freed slaves or their descendants and current governments, businesses, and individuals?" Any that existed and were broken should be open to a legal decision that's enforceable against the defendant. The Supreme Court's July 2020 ruling for the Creek Indians is an example. The Court upheld a claim to reservation jurisdiction in a large swath of Oklahoma that pre-dated Oklahoma's statehood. As a result, much of Tulsa, the state's second largest city, now finds itself on reservation land.

The 1860 U.S. Census shows that a mere 1.2% of the country's population held slaves then; do parties today have legal standing to seek a portion of wealth from descendants who have survived from those 384,884 slaveholders?[97] W.E.B. Du Bois recounts Dougherty County, GA, the former cornerstone of King Cotton that once counted ten thousand slaves and two thousand Whites. He tells readers that much of the wealth there didn't last a generation.[98] No, reparations activists will skip the original sinners and their heirs in search of deeper pockets and an easier target: the bottomless purse of the continuously-active federal government.

Governments could certainly be subject to providing redress if they entered into enforceable agreements, or, one may argue, if they were overtly complicit in allowing or facilitating such oppression. Are government's also responsible for preventing unethical schemes of immoral opportunistic hucksters like mortgage lenders (of any race or ethnicity) from scamming targets (of any race or ethnicity)? Reparations advocates want to claim they are and should be held accountable today.

As we've read, the earliest federal agreement with freed slaves was General William T. Sherman's Jan 16, 1865 field order providing freedmen's families 40 acres of land.[99]

Democrat President Andrew Johnson, however, returned the vast majority of that land to its original owners eight months later, leaving most freedmen the same as before: landless. While morally defective, Johnson's ruling was legal.

Then there's the matter of early federal programs for existing and potential homeowners that disregarded responsibilities to enforce the 14th Amendment. How should *that* be addressed?

Much of it *has* been addressed through the federally-legislated Civil Rights Act of 1964 and the Fair Housing Act of 1968; the government remains culpable for failures prior to that. Now, the onerous task follows of determining whose 14th Amendment rights the government neglected. Knowing the discriminatory policy in effect at that time, would Blacks have even bothered looking or applying for federally-insured housing? If not, how will the parties prove specific discrimination charges? Story-telling about individual infringements may be illustrative, but it's neither definitive nor conclusive evidence of wrongdoing.

Those thoughts figure into claims that the government should provide *all* Blacks some form of government redress. In view of how few people were actual slaveholders, is that fair to *all* of today's taxpayers? You could double or triple the number of slaveholders to account for offending overseers and such, and the proportion would still be below 5% of the population. How is it fair or reasonable to hold all of today's taxpayers accountable for what so few of some of their ancestors did 150 years ago?

Counting all taxpayers would also include descendants of Union soldiers who fought for slave freedom, abolitionists who actively and passionately campaigned against slavery, as well as the similarly-oppressed groups discussed in the previous section. Is it fair for their descendants to have to pay? Or should they get an exemption?

One response is that we all enjoy the blessings of past government, so all of us are also obliged to bear the burdens of correcting its past mistakes. Or, as Thomas Paine said, "Those who expect to reap the blessings of freedom must undergo the fatigue of supporting it."

Much of the answer lies in the form of the reparations.

#3. What Forms of Reparations Are Appropriate?

Any form of government redress must be both appropriate to a legal infringement and also practical to implement, with an ultimate goal of closing gaps between lingering impacts of prior violations and American ideals of liberty and justice for all.

While Du Bois' goal was to "... seek the social regeneration of the Negro", today's most outspoken activists are much more focused on monetary payments than eliminating lingering hurdles to social recognition. Some compare the average family wealth of black and white households to determine that a direct $175,000 payment per beneficiary from Whites is necessary to balance wealth. They also demand free college tuition, student loan forgiveness, home improvement grants, and liberal home loans.

Of note, none of their demands give any consideration to what taxpayers have already provided over the past 155 years since the Civil War, and that amount has been *very* considerable.

The cost of the federally-legislated Freedmen's Bureau itself, which provided food, shelter, clothing, medical and legal services, and land management over seven years, may have cost as much as $500 million in today's dollars.[100] The Bureau's chief, General Oliver Howard (for whom Howard University is named) himself disbursed $15m in Reconstruction-era dollars.

The *really* big bucks, though, have been in social programs that continue benefitting low-income people ever since President Lyndon Johnson launched "The Great Society" in the early 1960s. The number of original programs has multiplied to over 125 as of last year.

Federal and state governments spend about one *trillion* dollars annually on public assistance (commonly referred to as "welfare") through a combination of cash and cash-like benefits, means-tested health care, education, and job-training.[101] Since the Emancipation, many Blacks have become very successful and don't need any of these benefits. Unfortunately, about 8.1m other Blacks who comprise 24% of America's 2019 population in poverty do. They don't receive those benefits uniformly, but simple math shows the magnitude of government largesse: $1 trillion ÷ all 34m recipients = about $30,000 per person. And that's just for last year.

That's an enormous amount of redress for Americans who haven't moved beyond poverty on their own. When you add preferential admissions to higher education, job and promotion preferences in government and business, the demands for even more compensation become considerably weaker.

In all instances, though, it is incumbent upon governments to amend or repeal residual restrictions that deny equal opportunity and justice. Too many Asian, American Indian, and black minority members have embraced opportunity and risen above their former station. They are proof that people succeed when society removes discriminatory barriers. Others need some additional help.

Some of that help may be an initiative by the Ashville, NC city council this year that aims "to embed systemic solutions and go through a "reconciliation" process with its Black and Indigenous [PC for American Indians] residents.

 The measure calls for a plan to provide reparations to its black residents in the form of investments in their community such as increasing minority home ownership, increasing minority business ownership and career opportunities, and undertaking strategies to grow equity and generational wealth.[102]

Depending upon how it's funded, that approach may well be a very positive and practical solution on three counts. It is more inclusive of all disadvantaged community members, it directly addresses two major grievances (stolen slave labor and denied wealth-building), and it avoids the overly complex issues of who benefits. It'll be interesting to follow the programs to see how effective they are and how many are transferable elsewhere.

Beyond court judgments, the matter becomes one of morals, and outside the purview of government's legal responsibility. That doesn't preclude governments, however, from recognizing past immoral actions that were legal then and worthy of examination and ways to cure them in light of our national ideals.

I've Had Enough!

President Clinton's public recognition of and national apology for the government's culpability during the Tuskegee medical experiments serves as a useful guide for recognizing the plights of other Americans, their contributions, and subsequent injustices, as well as the country's continuous efforts to become a more perfect union. Similar events could be conducted for other groups who suffered from government neglect.

Another possibility is recognizing that members of *all* races and ethnicities have suffered injustices of the past, that cures have been enacted, and descendants must take advantage of them rather than demand taxpayers fund presumed, hoped for, but nonexistent family inheritances.

Given the myriad of complexities, claims, and counter-claims, the single best way forward is a sustained, robust economy that creates meaningful, well-paying jobs for every American seeking one. That enables them to build security and a better quality of life through personal savings, retirement plans, and desirable home ownership.

Parting Considerations

In an ironic contradiction, many black activists' fervent demands would create or revive their economic, employment, and social dependency on the very people they so ardently seek equality with: successful members of the majority. The alternative, of course, is to accelerate the way forward with their own human potential.

Future discussions will certainly look into Asians' success in adapting and assimilating while still retaining unique aspects of their culture. Other observers will wonder why too many Blacks haven't assimilated more successfully into mainstream society when a million legal immigrants do so every year. Discriminated populations elsewhere have also succeeded, such as the liberated prisoners from Nazi concentration and extermination camps. Or how East Germans successfully assimilated with more advanced West Berlin after the Berlin Wall toppled 30 years ago.

None of this amounts to a call to forget history, unique aspects of any race's, ethnicity's, or individuals' pasts. At the same time, though, people must be fully aware that in our highly-advanced society where human knowledge is doubling every 13 months, those past realities must be kept in proper perspective.[103] Excessive fixations on 158-year-old, six generations' ago tragedies and residual by-products at the expense of looking forward and taking advantage of current opportunities has a cost.

Popular black rap artist Kanye West, with over 750 artistic nominations and 255 awards, said in a 2018 TMZ interview, "You hear about slavery for 400 years…for 400 years? [Dwelling on] That sounds like a choice. Like, you was there for 400 years and it's all y'all? "You know like, it's like we're, we're mentally in prison. I like the word prison 'cause "slavery" goes too, too direct to the idea of blacks. It's like slavery, Holocaust. Holocaust – Jews. Slavery is black. So prison is something that unites us as one race – Blacks, and Whites being one race. Uh, that we're the human race."

Libs have been roundly degrading Kanye West for leaving the Democrat plantation with his independent thinking.

Minorities are quite aware of their racial pasts and what was denied them, but many of each race and ethnicity look to the future and take full advantage of what *is* available and successfully pursue their dreams. "Look up! If you don't look up, you can't get up," says a philosophical black free-holder.[104]

How long will it be, if ever, until all citizens identify themselves primarily as Americans?

I've Had Enough!

Chapter 10: "Racist!"

"Every great cause begins as a movement, becomes a business, and eventually degenerates into a racket."

Eric Hoffer, moral and social philosopher

T here's absolutely no question about it: National Basketball Association (NBA) referees are blatantly racist! You can't draw any other conclusion when black males aged 20-44 comprise only 4.6% of the general population but get called for 60% of the most personal fouls for the most seasons? Even worse, the top three players with the most personal fouls were *all* Black! [105] The officials have *got* to be racist, right?

In the NBA, black players, especially elite ones, dominate the sport and have more time on the court than white players. That simple reality is a critical consideration. If you calculated fouls-per-minute of playing time, you still may not reliably conclude that racism accounts for Blacks being penalized more than Whites. Did the black players actually *commit* more fouls - are some players simply more prone to fouling? It's much easier to promote a cause with simple associations, but they're seldom accurate.

Bullying and name-calling everyone who doesn't agree with you a "racist" is the automatic paragon that stands ahead of every other smear in the liberal playbook. It's what they scream when they want to paint others profoundly evil or just can't rationally respond to political challenges or different ideas. It's their go-to denunciation of any and all who dare confront any aspect of their ideology – it's the Holy Grail of retorts.

Even a perceived slight, however inadvertent or tenuously associated with race, triggers the indictment. It immediately terminates further discussion and covers their intellectual retreat into a protective cocoon of ignorant self-righteousness. Liberals are drawn to racial identity politics like moths to flames – the automatic pull is relentless, overwhelming, and inescapable. The obsession both quenches and ignites their emotions and launches ever more protests, demands, studies, and programs.

I've Had Enough!

Liberals and race-baiters are equally quick to scream "racism!" when minorities are disproportionately represented (such as incarcerations), unless it's in activities where they successfully abound like pro basketball, football, and certain music genres. But is race really the fundamental basis of all of their habitually-concluded racism?

Too often there is an easily-observed relationship between a situation and race that is a *correlation* rather than *causation*. Let's look at the two terms. If you see that drowning deaths increased with the consumption of ice tea, you may quickly and erroneously conclude that ice tea was responsible for that uptick in deaths. Too many liberals habitually think like that, not recognizing one or more other critical factors. In this case, hot summer weather is much more responsible for both activities. There is a *correlation* between increased ice tea consumption and drowning deaths, but neither activity is the *cause* of the other.

In 2012, major mortgage lenders steered many urban Blacks into loans with significantly higher interest charges than the lower rates more than a few of them could've qualified for. The nation's largest mortgage lender that year, Wells Fargo, settled one resultant lawsuit with Baltimore, MD for $175 million, and committed to investing more than $400 million in response to a lawsuit in the Memphis, TN region. The Cook County, IL District Attorney filed discrimination charges against lenders in 2014. The U.S. Department of Justice settled other such claims with Countrywide Financial and SunTrust Mortgage, which paid $300m and $12m in damages respectively.[106]

Was racism the key motivation behind these lending practices? In other words, was the primary intent of the many bank officers to harm people just because they were Black? Or, like the tea and drowning example above, was another factor at play... in this case, simple old-fashioned greed? Is it more likely they preyed on *anyone* who was financially illiterate *regardless* of their race? Here, the relationship between financially inexperienced victims and color appears to be much more a correlation than a cause. Nevertheless, the targets happened to *be* Black and Hispanic, so prosecutors charged the banks with *racial* discrimination.

Predatory lending experiences should have also brought intense public attention to the immorality of those banks' officers and the lack of financial literacy taught in schools. Roughly 1 in 5 U.S. 15-year-olds don't understand basic financial concepts. [107]

There is another attribute that more consistently and broadly stands behind and enables so many abuses now catalogued as racist, and that attribute is *power*. Power can be physical, intellectual, and financial. It also comes in the forms of political and business influence. College officials have it in the form of admissions, grades, and approval of PhD theses. Hollywood producer Harvey Weinstein held immense power in the form of script and role approvals. Government, businesses, and universities lost significant power in the 1960's when their conduct undermined their moral authority.

Regardless of its form, individuals and groups with less power are invariably beset by those with more, and *all races and ethnicities have been on both sides of power differences*. Society's challenge is to strike a precautionary balance between those who wield it and those who don't. In the lending example, greed was the motivation, but power enabled its fulfillment.

Previous chapters presented major historical factors affecting population failures and success from abusive Jim Crow laws, financing practices, and government housing programs, to academic breakdowns. These and other one-sided practices were conducted by those who *had* power against those who *didn't*. This is an important distinction from racial identities for three reasons. First, it recognizes that race alone isn't what makes someone an oppressor or oppressed, even though media, academics, and activists continually assume it is. It should be obvious that none of the laws, events, and injustices were imposed by all members of one race on all members of another.

Second, the distinction focuses on the fact that *power* is the root prerequisite for tyranny and oppression, as discussed in Chapter 9. Power held by some (immoral) people regardless of race leads to discrimination, abuse, and worse against other races as well as their own. Finally, for those who want to effect change, it spotlights the necessity of actually obtaining and exercising power, instead of just displacing one race with another that can be just as prone to abuse (as seen in Baltimore's succession of minority mayors).

I've Had Enough!

Anyone familiar with American history would certainly conclude that a large number of, but not all, powerful people who
wronged Blacks were, indeed, White. And yes, in addition to harm-
ing many powerless who were Black, they also brought benefits to
a number of Whites (some of it assisted by government housing actions cited in Chapter 5 and passing to descendants).

Barack and Michelle Obama's power gained them privilege
above just about every other family in America. Ditto for other powerful Blacks. Fortunately for the less-powerful, the proportion of
Blacks earning middle-class annual incomes of $50 - $150k has
risen from 22% to 36% from 1967 to 2018, and the proportion earning under $15-$25k dropped from 45% to 32% during the same
period.[108]

This doesn't suggest there aren't any racial bigots of every
stripe, there certainly are, regardless of their relative power. Overall,
though, categorically naming race as the basis for differentiating
victims from perpetrators sidelines or submerges more productive
actions.

Promoting a racial focus allows liberals to stir the pot for
their own power plays. For example, they can much more easily cast
the roles of good guy and bad guy as those who conform to their
dogma vs. everyone else. Then-presidential candidate Joe Biden told
his black radio talk show host, "Well, I tell you what, if you have a
problem figuring out whether you're for me or Trump, then you ain't
Black."

It also greatly simplifies recruiting chores: "If you're Black,
you're oppressed – join me in the fight against the white majority"
is infinitely easier to convey than the more truthful, "If a greedy sub-
prime lender used his more powerful financial knowledge to take
advantage of your financial ignorance, join my campaign against
them and to improve your financial literacy".

Liberal elites, their think tanks, and sycophantic zealots have
taken racism to new heights, moving from reality to fantasy. And if
you commit one of their many perceived transgressions, you're the
immediate and unrelenting target of every racial re-education officer, inclusion board and counsellor they can bring to bear. Which
is one reason Whites distance themselves from closer work,

recreational, or social occasions where they'd ordinarily include minorities.

From experience...

In 1998 I deployed with the U.S. 3rd Army HQ to Kuwait in response to Saddam Hussein's threat to shoot down the UN's surveillance aircraft. There, I noticed a newly-attached black female major on my staff who was very active but equally unproductive. She had a cheery attitude and was constantly moving about, but never made meaningful contributions to the many requirements that poured in hourly. I penned her a note listing observed strengths, shortfalls, and suggested improvements.

The following morning there was a very defensive response sitting on my desk; she'd taken my communication much more personally than professionally. She also stated that no one else had ever criticized her performance.

The next day I called her into my office to clear the air face-to-face. To stay focused on performance and standards, I'd prepared a number of examples that compared her activities with expectations of her rank. She was receptive and listened. Within minutes, she looked up and said, "Colonel Ross, I understand."

Saddam didn't shoot at the UN aircraft, the tactical situation abated, and I rotated back to the states, wondering why no former leader had mentored her. I can only assume that they were reluctant to critique a black female officer, no matter how well-intentioned, for fear of arousing a lengthy, defamatory, racial-sexual bias complaint against them.

Those same defensive instincts kick-in around business offices, too. "Should we include the minority/female/gay co-workers to lunch today, or will they interpret a remark or action as biased and bring a ton of time-consuming interviews, interrogations, and mandatory sensing/awareness sessions down on us?" It's so much easier to go by themselves, which the minority/female/gay co-worker also interprets as discriminatory. Lose-lose.

If Whites move out of a neighborhood, it's white flight; if they stay, it's gentrification. If they see color, it's automatically racism; if they don't see color, they're ignoring racism. Whites who engage black culture are guilty of appropriation; if they ignore black culture they're non-inclusive. Liberals can spin anything into racism to arouse emotions for support.

Of course, racism also works the other way. Civil rights activist Jesse Jackson famously told The Washington Post reporter Milton Coleman during an interview that touched on Jews, "That's all Hymie wants to talk about is Israel. Every time you go to Hymietown that's all they want to talk about." Per protocol, Jackson ritualistically apologized to Jews but some remained skeptical of his sincerity. Human nature is color blind.

Other powerful minorities also abuse their position. After leftist billionaire George Soros pumped $2m into a Political Action Committee that spent over $570k on costs to oppose Kim Foxx's chief opponent, black liberal female Foxx was elected as the Cook County, IL (Chicago) District Attorney.[109] Using that position during a high-profile case, she dropped all charges against black actor Jussie Smollett for filing false police reports. Cook County Circuit Judge Michael Toomin subsequently appointed a special prosecutor to reopen the DA's investigation. The Cook County Board of Commissioners President and Chair of the Cook County Democrat Party Toni Preckwinkle pushed to unseat the judge in November, despite his 40 years on the bench and support by all major bar associations (voters re-elected him in November, 2020).

Black female District Attorney Kim Gardner of St. Louis, MO charged a white couple who were holding firearms on the porch to defend themselves and their property. They were inside a gated community protecting their home from a shouting mob of Black Lives Matter protesters who'd broken the gates. The McCloskeys fired no shots, yet Gardner charged the couple for unlawful use of a weapon. George Soros poured $116k into the Missouri Safety and Justice committee, which helped Gardner's 2020 re-election campaign to the tune of over $77,000.[110]

Another Soros campaign beneficiary, black female DA Diana Becton of Contra Costa, CA had a couple arrested for a hate crime when they painted over street graffiti (a BLM sign). In another decision, she wants the police to determine if looters needed stolen goods prior to charging them for stealing.[111]

R.J. Ross

Racism is a scourge that race hucksters want audiences to believe is exclusive to Whites, but UNC Associate Professor Tressie McMillan Cottom proved them wrong again with this tweet;

The larger issue here is why the University of North Carolina administration didn't summarily fire Cotton for spreading such an inflammatory racist delusion? How can they allow someone with a perversly-biased temperment to stand before a room full of students? Where is the University Office for Diversity and Inclusion in this blatant racial attack and affront to common sense and human sensibilities? That office, the President, and board are no doubt staffed with leftists.

Institutional Bias. Federal, state, and municipal governments have clearly been guilty of racial discrimination against minorities as detailed in Chapter 5.

As shown earlier, housing discrimination against minorities was an especially pernicious issue. The federal government finally responded with the Fair Housing Act, whose foundation was the even broader federal Civil Rights Act of 1964. The next year the president signed into law the 1965 Voter Rights Act.

As a result of these key federal laws, people throughout the country have clear grounds to legally challenge discriminatory conduct by individuals, businesses, institutions, and governments; if the challenged leaders don't stop the purported violations, take them to court. The NAACP is always willing to pursue such cases.

The laws resulted in significant progress towards achieving the American ideal for all, but there's always work to do. Efforts continued this year when the Federal Reserve took a step to update its rules for the 1977 Community reinvestment Act (CRA), which is aimed at keeping banks from avoiding investments in lower-income neighborhoods. The Fed seeks to coordinate CRA updates with the Treasury, which oversees about 70% of activity under low-income lending rules, to reduce conflicting guidance to banks.[112]

Significantly, mega-bank JPMorgan unveiled in October 2020 a $30 *billion* five-year program focused heavily on expanding Black and Latino access to housing and boosting minority-owned businesses. Giant firms Apple, Google, and others are also pledging hundreds of millions of dollars to initiatives to help offset past inequities.

Education. Liberals, especially those in higher education, will go to any extreme and create any rationale for their student body to mirror the racial mixture at-large (even in small niches where it's all but impossible). They don't do the hard, essential work to actually *qualify* minorities, but the much easier virtue signaling that's become absolutely necessary nowadays to avert peer accusations of racism. They'll cite discriminatory impacts of low-income parents who couldn't afford tutors, culturally-biased testing, and a variety of other external factors. What they *won't* entertain is any minority student's failures in high school, such as completing all homework, reading more, taking advanced placement or summer classes. If minority students are less academically prepared, no problem – just lower the standards or make up criteria to reevaluate their application and raise their admissions rankings.

Federal judge Allison D. Burroughs decided in Harvard's favor against an Asian students' 2019 lawsuit that charged the university with discriminatory admissions standards. Harvard incorporates subjective "personal ratings" that favor applicants with lower academic credentials. Rather than have Harvard defend the lower personal ratings it assigns to Asians, Burroughs held that the plaintiffs hadn't proven the lower ratings resulted from animus by Harvard officials. Apparently, she concluded that Harvard apparently didn't want to *hurt* Asians, but just favor other minorities – as if Harvard's rejection didn't deliberately and negatively affect Asians.

This year, 2020, the federal Department of Justice filed a lawsuit against Yale University, charging that its undergraduate admissions policy discriminates on the basis of race. Per its investigation, Asian and white Americans have "only one-tenth to one-fourth of the likelihood of admission as African American applicants with comparable academic credentials." Assistant Attorney General Eric Dreiband, who runs the department's civil rights division: "All persons who apply for admission to colleges and universities should expect and know that they will be judged by their character, talents, and achievements and not the color of their skin. To do otherwise is to permit our institutions to foster stereotypes, bitterness, and division."

Liberals argue that Blacks face a White Euro-centric culture and admissions criteria that ignore or diminish their own unique values. America's aspirational values and the behaviors behind the nation's success have stood the test of millennia and are irrespective of race, gender, and faith. This will be discussed more thoroughly in Chapter 14.

Over centuries, our very diverse population evolved an *American* culture more than it has any national white, black, Asian, Middle-Eastern, Hispanic, Indian, or Pacific Islander one. It also happens to be a collective culture that's proven more successful than any other before it (see Chapter 16 for a discussion of success), and much of the successful innovation, problem-solving, administration, and maintenance of our more intricate activities comes from college graduates.

Isn't it just common sense, then, to test applicants' preparation for the more demanding studies that contribute to our collective success? If minority students aspiring to college are underrepresented because they're inadequately prepared, then preparedness is the issue. It may be due to grade 1-12 teachers, programs, facilities, and supplies, or it may be due to their cultural attitude toward education (a factor that libs won't even consider). Blaming it on the height of the goalposts is cowardly, mis-directed pandering.

Liberals are absolutely correct on one point, though: there *is* a large and persistent academic difference between average black and other test-takers. The largest difference is between Blacks and another very visually-distinctive race, Asians. Asians assuredly endured their share of oppression and discrimination, yet still do extremely well academically.

Administrators of the standardized SAT college admissions test report that significant test score differences have been consistent for years, as exemplified by results for the high school class of 2020;

SAT Performance, 2019 [113]

	Mean Score			Benchmark Met			
	Total	ERW	Math	Both	ERW	Math	None
All	1059	531	528	45%	68%	48%	30%
Asians	1223	586	637	**75%**	83%	80%	**11%**
Whites	1114	562	553	57%	80%	59%	18%
Hispanic	978	495	483	29%	55%	31%	43%
Blacks	933	476	457	**20%**	46%	22%	**53%**

Note: the College Board web site provides a link students can use to take a free practice test

Asian family and student culture must place a greater premium on education and it's clearly reflected in their consistently higher performance on this widely-accepted standardized tests used to assess high school students' academic preparation for college.

While some other minorities default to complaining that exams are biased against their heritage and racial culture, Asian students study material that is imperative for success in our sophisticated society: the ability to communicate effectively to a broad audience through the written word, reading and understanding what others have written, and mathematics – a language extensively used in business, engineering, science, and sociology.

Yet, liberals persist in their equal-outcome campaigns despite truths in front of their faces. Liberal opponents of college admissions tests criticize the tests for failing to consider traits like interpersonal relationships and creativity. Measuring those factors is open to extremely arbitrary scoring, which is their point. It provides the back door to beef up overall scores of applicants who are academically underprepared.

I suppose they also "know" that minority applicants are innately more creative and form more effective interpersonal relationships than Asians and Whites. Otherwise, those scores would all be equivalent and they'd be back to square one.

In May 2020, the University of California's Board of Regents went so far as to completely suspend major admission test requirements for freshmen through 2024 and eliminate them afterwards.[114] This major change didn't even offer a substitute methodology to determine which of the many applicants the university would accept, but it needs to figure one out soon. UC admission rates for fall 2020 ranged from 14.4% of applicants to the Los Angeles campus and 17.5% to Berkeley to a high of 90.8% at Merced; the average admit rate was 69.2%.[115]

Said another way. No matter how well developed their agricultural skills, successful wheat farmers won't thrive in a Silicon Valley IT development job without learning and effectively applying appropriate technical skills. If Midwestern farmers are underrepresented in IT development, it isn't because tech companies discriminate against people in bib overalls. Energizing some National Association of Frustrated Farmers to help force the tech world to revolve around farmers' agricultural skills and behaviors isn't the solution either.

Conversely, information technology wonks won't produce a bountiful harvest on an Iowa farm without knowing and practicing appropriate agricultural skills.

Income and Wealth. Given their academic preparation to obtain advanced skills rewarded in our economy, it's no surprise that many Asians' accomplishments are recognized with significantly higher incomes.

Estimated Household Income, 2002 – 2018 [116]

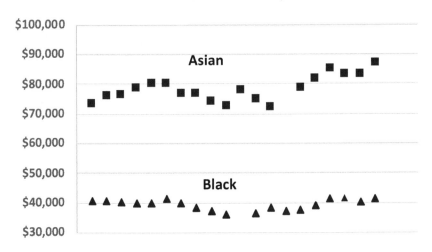

At the other end of the income scale, Asians' education and work-ethic contribute to their much smaller proportion in poverty.

% of Each Race Below Poverty, 2002 – 2018 [117]

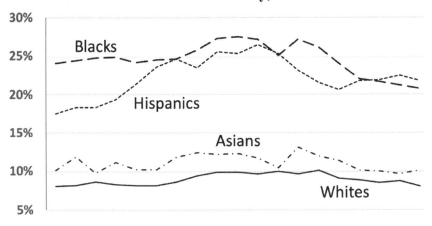

Another key financial measure with broad racial differences is family wealth. That wealth can provide a degree of economic security in the event of financial adversities like job loss or a major health expense. It can fund higher education or a down payment on a house – preferably in a secure neighborhood with good schools. Financial security can ease the risks of a job change or starting your own business.

Major contributing factors to wealth include education level, consumption vs. savings ability and practices, parents' wealth, and age (older people tend to have acquired more). Discrimination has played a role in a number of Blacks' opportunities to build wealth, starting with the denied 40 acres of land and moving on to the numerous federal, state, city, and neighborhood restrictions on where they could buy houses and how they could finance them.

That, in turn, consigned many of their children to inferior schools. Discrimination by unions and the government's failure to stop it relegated many WWII-era Blacks to lower-paying jobs, education, income, and home-buying – all key to building wealth. That, in turn, affects the wealth that families can pass on to descendants. The total effect of all these factors can be significant. Illegal aliens who compete for jobs, particularly lower-skilled ones, can also impact Americans' ability to build wealth. Absent that labor in a robust economy, employers have to increase wages to obtain scarce labor – which builds wealth.

Family wealth is generally concentrated in four categories.[118]

HOME OWNERSHIP is one of the biggest components of family wealth, with the potential to appreciate significantly, particularly houses in high-performing school districts. 2019 ownership rates are much higher for middle-age Whites than Blacks (73% vs. 51%), as are typical home values: $230,000 for Whites, $200,000 for Hispanics, and $150,000 for Blacks. Interestingly, the 'Other' category of races' typical value is $310,000. Differences may be due to income and down payments, segregation, and age of entry into home ownership.

RETIREMENT ACCOUNTS generally account for the next largest segment of family wealth. They may be employer-sponsored plans (defined benefit pensions or defined contribution 401(k) type plans) or independent of an employer (an IRA). All plans are sensitive to how much is put into them, how contributions are invested, the economy, and their longevity. Again, there are large racial differences in retirement account eligibility and participation.

Among middle-aged families (who have the highest rates of account ownership), 65% of Whites have at least one account compared to 44% of Blacks and 28% of Hispanic families. One reason for the disparity is eligibility: some employers don't offer plans at all, don't offer them to part-time employees, or the employee lacks tenure on the job.

Participation in eligible plans also varies: about 90% of eligible white and other families participate, 80% of black families and 75% of Hispanic families do. Participation factors include having sufficient income, types of employer funds, whether participation is by default or not, and financial literacy.

Finally, account balances also vary for working-age families that have them. Here, the typical white family has about $50,000; typical black and Hispanic families have about $20,000. Other families have a median balance of $34,000. Most workers, of course, will also receive Social Security benefits in retirement.

An interesting question is to what extent the legacy of the failed Freedman's Savings and Trust Company had on prior and current Blacks' confidence in financial institutions that hold and manage retirement accounts?

INTER-GENERATIONAL TRANSFERS come in the form of outright monetary gifts, help with educational expenses and house or vehicle down payments, and inheritances. "Careful economic studies actually demonstrate that inheritances, bequests and intrafamily transfers account for more of the racial wealth gap than any other demographic and socioeconomic indicators including education, income, and household structure."[119]

The number of families that have received an inheritance varies substantially by race: White, 30%; Other, 18%; Black, 10%; Hispanic, 7%. Of those families that received an inheritance, the median amounts were less skewed: Whites, $89,000; Blacks, $86,000, Hispanic, $52,000, and Other, $59,000.

SAVINGS/OTHER INVESTMENTS provide an immediate source of funds for unexpected expenses and disruptions to income. Nearly all families have some type of highly-liquid assets, like a checking or savings account or a pre-paid card. Here again, though, the Board of Governors of the Federal Reserve reports differences in their amounts. The typical white family held about $8,000 vs. $1,500 for Blacks and $2,000 for Hispanics. Families in the Other category held about $5,000.

Since wealth is accumulated over years or generations, it'll be useful to learn what differences emerge from the impacts of the economic and employment upsurge through early 2020 and the off-setting COVID-19 virus impacts afterwards.

When viewed across the range of power - who's held it and still does - wealth is quite expectedly distributed accordingly. Studies show that the disparities have existed over time, stages of life, and education and income levels. Racially, Hispanics are closing the gap with Whites.

There is a range of proposals to more closely balance wealth differences, with liberals favoring much more blunt approaches. Economists Darrick Hamilton and William Darity Jr. advance the idea of 'baby bonds'- a direct government-enforced distribution of family wealth. The federal government would establish a trust for every American newborn, progressively funded up to $50,000 or $60,000 depending on their family's wealth at birth and earning 1.5% - 2% per year. Recipients could access the money at age 18.

They estimate the total annual cost at about $60 billion, but studies cited to support their premises are 10 to 31 years old.

A taxpayer-funded, government managed baby trust would be fraught with likely abuses by candidates promising ever more benefits and government officials who decide who gets how much, as well as scammers eager to serve as 'agents' to help recipients navigate government forms and investment choices. How long would it take politicians to 'borrow' the initial fund balances and their earnings to subsidize 'emergency' or favorite projects (think about Social Security reserves)?

Liberals salivate at the prospect of even more direct measures to re-allocate slices of the existing 'wealth pie' through new taxes on inheritances (which have already been taxed when they were earned), existing wealth (which has also been taxed once), and capital income. Those centrally-directed actions would temporarily appease the beneficiaries but rightfully infuriate families targeted to pay for the programs.

The competing vision is to *grow the size of the whole pie*, eliminate unnecessary government constraints on new entrepreneurs and existing businesses so they can hire more workers, pay higher wages, and enlarge and broaden our national economy. It would also be beneficial to encourage minority businessmen to open more banks, which traditionally serve more minority clients.

A vigorously growing economy is the most practical avenue to building wealth for the most people. Families then earn the means to participate in retirement programs, save for a rainy day, get into a home, and build more for their children's future.

Crime rates are one more vital measure of racial differences, especially those for violent crimes. The differences go a long way to explaining why police kill more Blacks than Whites (details in the next chapter).

Arrests per 100k Population, 2017 [120]

	Murder	Rape	Agg. Aslt.	Robbery
Blacks	127	131	2,574	1,015
Hispanics	26	26	1,081	225
Whites	21	62	953	163
Asians	7	18	287	39

Why are Asians so much less involved in crime than Blacks?

Implicit Bias. In 1988 social psychologists Anthony Greenwald and Mahzarrin Banaji developed their Implicit Association Test, an image-reaction exercise that they purport identifies unconscious bias against Blacks and can predict discriminatory behavior.

Liberals trot out this concept with regularity when they can't identify actual bias in college acceptance rates, hiring, promotion and firing choices, elections, and just about every other life event whose outcome they object to. Research author Heather Mac Donald completely dismantles their claims in her work <u>The Diversity Delusion</u>.

Leftists also rail their enemies for stereotyping Blacks for traits that W.E.B. Du Bois observed in 1903: poor, ignorant, plodding, and to a degree shiftless. He goes on to explain that they were not *inherently* so, but were through culture and experience. That raises the question, "Can't the current truths depicted in the charts above influence *other* people's racial impressions?" Yes, it can and does.

Stereotypes are preconceived notions about people's behaviors, capabilities, and characteristics that we use to more easily and rapidly judge the hundreds of people we deal with every day: associates, students, clerks, professionals, folks in the news, you name it. Absent the time to know them individually, we often rely on such notions. Sometimes they are accurate time-saving means to quickly get into matters-at-hand, not harmful or even detrimental to either party. Other times, of course, a rush to judgment is erroneous and possibly harmful. What broad stereotypes do many people associate with a number of black people, and why?

During the Jim Crow era, Blacks crossed to the other side of the street to avoid proximity with a White; nowadays, Whites cross the road to avoid a couple of hooded Blacks. What brought about the reversal? Could a black murder rate 6x that of Whites be relevant? That's certainly not to say that every Black, or even a predominant proportion of those in hoodies and talking loudly, has a criminal record and is intent on expanding it. But people's uncertainties and their instinct for survival combined with frightening crime numbers certainly figure into such behaviors.

Another prevalent stereotype regards education. While many Blacks are brilliant (the oft-referenced W.E.B. Du Bois in this book, for example, and 2020 Rhodes Scholars GA Phaidra Buchanan and Sam Patterson from Atlanta, and among the most intellectually capable among us, Blacks as a race consistently lag in standardized tests as shown earlier. Any attitudes some of them may express about class participation, study, and homework and "being White"

I've Had Enough!

only promote the stereotype and contradict the intense passion freed slaves had for knowledge.

These and other interracial stereotypes beg the question of how to diminish or eradicate them.

"...[discrimination] must be solved in the homes of every American in every community across our country."
President John F. Kennedy

In a nutshell, the underlying conducts have to change and that may well take a generation or two. For more, see Chapter 15.

In the spirit of the Scots of old, here's a remarkable example of change from our own past.

American Indian tribes dominated the central United States for centuries prior to settlers encroaching westward onto that same land. The fiercest of all the Plains tribesmen were the Comanches. The largest, most powerful Comanche band, the Penatekas, increasingly came in contact with white traders and eventually signed treaties relegating them to reservations. They were followed by the Yamparika, Kotoseka, and Nokoni bands. The fifth Comanche band, the Quahadis were hardened holdouts who never signed a treaty.

The Quahadi's greatest leader was Quanah Parker, young son of Chief Peta Nocona and his captured white settler bride Cynthia Ann Parker. Quanah was renowned among the Comanche bands, the combative Kiowas, and his U.S. Army adversaries for unparalleled bravery, and tactical acumen. After all the other bands had capitulated, Quanah continued to lead raids on homesteads and against cavalry units. As the Indian Wars moved into 1875, however, even the relentless Quanah reconsidered his people's future.

To everyone's immense surprise, he changed – significantly, pivoting 180° from a primeval plains warrior to a tax-paying entrepreneur in industrializing America. As miraculous as that was, he did it without forsaking his people's long and storied past. Quanah became an excellent student of the new world that was sweeping his former vast hunting grounds and turned his knowledge and instincts to the Quahadis' advantage. He became such a force within the prevailing culture that he hosted President Theodore Roosevelt at his dinner table (and pressed him for more equity for his people).

Change has been done, can be done, and Blacks must lead it. One component should be a very public campaign showcasing past and present leaders who've risen above racial challenges, such as the Tuskegee Airmen, businessmen, artists, athletes, and government leaders.

Strong, admired, black leaders, with support from governments, businesses, and public figures, must lead the way in the models of Quanah Parker, W.E.B. Du Bois, Booker T. Washington, and Dr. Martin Luther King – rebuilding black families, promoting education, shunning crime, and demonstrating through example who they are and what they can achieve.

They must attack illiteracy and significantly reduce Black-on-Black murder and other criminal activity. Their followers will impress society-at-large with manner, thinking, and accomplishments that distinguish them from past stereotypes, to be embraced as neighbors, co-workers, spouses, and fellow Americans. Black writer Delano Squires says as much in his July 2020 article "It's Time for The Conversation About Black Lives To Stop Focusing On White People". Black author and activist Robert "Bob" Woodson is behind a very successful neighborhood transition from routine violence to no murders for 12 years, which he lead through direct interaction with its residents. The President awarded him the Presidential Citizens Medal for his work of over 40 years.[121]

Actor and rapper O'Shea Jackson (Ice Cube) has a Contract With Black America to address systemic issues, notably, the wealth gap, facing the black community. He's open to meeting with the next administration to coordinate an action plan that includes federal participation. Marcus Owens recently co-founded and leads the Black Business Support Collective Minnesota's Twin Cities to support black businesses. Who will join them or start their own campaign?

CEO and author Kathleen Brush concludes in her worldwide history of racism, "… the United States was [centuries ago] and remains the leading anti-racist nation."

I've Had Enough!

Chapter 11: Criminality

I n 1951, reporter Robert M. Yoder asked famous American bank robber Willie Sutton why he robbed banks. According to Yoder, a surprised Sutton responded, "Because that's where the money is."

Like the reporter, liberals constantly ask, "Why do the police kill such a disproportionate number of blacks?" and "Why are there so many more black inmates than Whites when Blacks comprise a much smaller proportion of the population?" The answer, to paraphrase Willie Sutton, is "Because they commit so many more crimes - especially violent crimes."

Liberals despise that response and refuse to acknowledge it, but we can learn the truth by examining national-level data bases. As expected, the voluminous amounts of particulars don't correlate exactly and each source presents its information somewhat differently. Together, however, they paint a compelling picture about race, crime, and police killings.

The Washington Post newspaper's Fatal Force Database. The Post was concerned that the FBI undercounted the number of people shot by the police, so it's maintained its own database of police line-of-duty killings since 2015. It's sourced by news accounts, social media postings, police reports, and by monitoring independent databases such as *Killed by Police* and *Fatal Encounters*.

Law enforcement officers may be federal agents, state police, state highway patrol, county sheriffs, or municipal police. Special jurisdiction police at airports, schools, subways, and government buildings are also considered.

On their police-shootings website, The Post prominently displays a bar graph showing the population size of racial/ethnic groups and the rate that each race is killed by the police. The dramatic pictorial drives their key point home with the statement, "The rate at which **black Americans are killed by police** is more than twice as high as **the rate for white Americans**" (emphasis on original).[122] That graph and statement should get every American's attention and ignite an interest to dig deeper. ___

Importantly, however, the website doesn't present any of the Post's collected data about the threat those police faced, which is a critical consideration. Examining that data as of Dec 5, 2020 shows that in 67% of the cases, victims were attacking, which the Post says, "… includes incidents where officers or others were shot at, threatened with a gun, attacked with other weapons or physical force, etc. The attack category is meant to flag the highest level of threat."

That, America, is crucial information regarding encounters that resulted in a fatal shooting by police.

The Post uses the threat title "Other" to describe circumstances of an additional 28% of Blacks and 30% of Whites killed by the police, which it says, "… includes many incidents where officers or others faced significant threats."

Finally, The Post lists as "Undetermined" 5% of the threat levels, or 61 cases, where police killed Blacks.[123] The proportion of Whites and Blacks who were armed was 94% and 91% respectively.

A separate category is "Fleeing" (Blacks, 43%; Whites 33%), which the newspaper explains, "The threat column and the fleeing column are not necessarily related. For example, there is an incident in which the suspect is moving away from officers (fleeing) and at the same time turns to fire a gun at the officer. Also, attacks represent a status immediately before fatal shots by police; while fleeing could begin slightly earlier and involve a chase."

These flagrant omissions are a significant breach of journalistic integrity, blatant bias, and an inflammatory example of liberal racism. But the Post also omitted any mention of some other revealing information that's highly relevant to the discussion. For that, turn to the Federal Bureau of Investigation (FBI).

FBI Uniform Crime Reporting Program. This exhaustive data source relies on voluntary participation by 15,000 of the nation's 18,700 law enforcement departments (some choose or are unable to participate). Departments range in size from one to 30,000 members. The Program has very detailed annual reports on crime and the number of police officers killed by the offenders' race, ethnicity, and sex. They're readily available online and are

R.J. Ross

downloadable as a pdf and/or Excel spreadsheet; complete reports lag by about 12-18 months.

At the time of this writing, The Washington Post data covered the period 2015 – Dec 5, 2020, so I selected an FBI annual report for 2017, the middle of the Post's period and graphed the comparative violent crime arrest rates for Blacks and Whites.

The FBI crime reporting tables provide some particularly revealing insights into the disproportionate rates that police kill members of the two races: their utterly disproportionate crime rates.

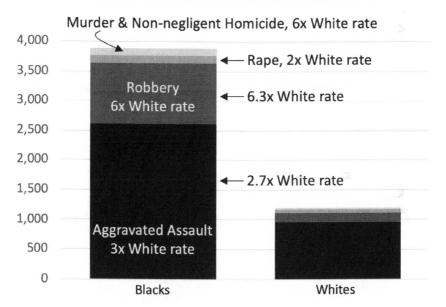

Blacks are arrested for violent crimes (murder, non-negligent manslaughter, rape, robbery, and aggravated assault) at *3.2x the rate of Whites and are arrested for murder at 6x the rate of Whites.* Observers would have to conclude that Blacks' involvement in violent crimes at such a greater rate is the primary factor in their being killed at a greater rate. For non-violent crimes, they're arrested at 1.9x the rate of Whites.

I've Had Enough!

Why doesn't The Washington Post, a major national newspaper, provide *that* information to balance and explain the disproportionate number of police killings? Blacks also kill police officers at almost 3x the rate as Whites do.[124]

As a check, the Federal Bureau of Prisons reports that blacks are federal inmates at 3.3x the rate of Whites, which closely parallels their rate of arrests for violent crimes.

The Centers for Disease Control maintains its own National Violent Death Reporting System (NVDRS) to record the number of such occurrences in the country along with descriptive information. Their data reflects a similar proportion of homicide/legal intervention deaths of Blacks and Whites.[125]

2018, United States
Homicide/Legal Intervention Injury Deaths and Rates per 100,000
Black, Non-Hispanic Both Sexes, All Ages
ICD-10 Codes: X85-Y09, Y87.1,Y35, Y89.0,*U01-*U02

Number of Deaths	Population	Crude Rate	Age-Adjusted Rate**
9,680	42,934,826	22.55	21.91

2018, United States
Homicide/Legal Intervention Injury Deaths and Rates per 100,000
White, Non-Hispanic Both Sexes, All Ages
ICD-10 Codes: X85-Y09, Y87.1,Y35, Y89.0,*U01-*U02

Number of Deaths	Population	Crude Rate	Age-Adjusted Rate**
5,838	201,068,278	2.90	2.98

The National Institutes of Health, the federal government's primary agency responsible for biomedical and public health research, also maintains records of deaths. Its National Violent Death Reporting System includes data from 17 states over the four years 2009-2012.

What's notable among all of the discussions and presentations is a failure of government leaders – the president, governors, mayors, city councils, police chiefs – to put crime numbers into perspective as they highlight events and interpretations that support their political agenda. When reporter Will Witt asked three young black men how many unarmed Blacks were killed by the police in 2019, they responded between 1,000 – 1,400. The number at that time was actually 9.[126]

Another failure is the lack of public and government leaders' support for law enforcement: failure to recognize their challenges, workload, and vastly overall outstanding performance. They uniformly avoid encouraging our best people from choosing a career in law enforcement.

Finally, very few leaders, be they elected, sports, business, or entertainment, make any point of spearheading national, state, and city campaigns to promote youngsters staying in school, avoiding illegal activity, and respecting proper authority.

I've Had Enough!

Chapter 12: Flash Points

O n Sunday afternoon, August 23, 2020, police in Kenosha, WI responded to a domestic violence call. As seen in a by-stander's video, two officers attempted to apprehend a black man who was walking around the front of his SUV. As the suspect opened the driver's side door and leaned in, an officer shot him in the back seven times. A witness told a TV news station the officers were yelling at the man to drop a knife.

Wisconsin's Democrat Governor Tony Evers quickly tweeted, "Tonight, Jacob Blake was shot in the back multiple times, in broad daylight, in Kenosha, Wisconsin. Kathy and I join his fam-ily, friends, and neighbors in hoping earnestly that he will not succumb to his injuries. While we do not have all of the details yet, what we know for certain is that he is not the first Black man or person to have been *shot or injured or mercilessly killed at the hands of individuals in law enforcement* in our state or our country." Em-phasis added.

He was exactly right to say "...we do not have all the details yet...", but would have been much more correct to say that he had *no* details or if he did, that he failed to acknowledge them. The gov-ernor's highly inflammatory statement about black men being "mercilessly killed at the hands... of law enforcement" is uncon-scionable when he, as the state's senior elected official, should have been supporting law and order, calling for restraint, and directing an immediate, thorough, transparent investigation of the actions and everyone involved in them. To liberals, though, it's whatever it takes to go along with the movement...

If Governor Evers had gathered some critical facts, he'd have learned that a black relative called the police because Blake "wasn't supposed to be there" (due to a restraining order). The po-lice knew Blake was a felon and attempted to arrest him after he'd just sexually assaulted his girlfriend. Blake failed to comply with officers' legal instructions and resisted arrest as bystanders warned "He's got a knife."

Despite being tasered, Blake broke away from the officers and moved around the front of his parked vehicle. He opened the driver-side door and leaned in. Fearing he was reaching for a lethal weapon, officer Rusten Sheskey shot Blake in the back multiple times (police found a knife on the floorboard). An ambulance took Blake to a hospital where he recovered, but is currently paralyzed from the waist down.

Absent a clarifying update by the governor or responsible media, protesters believed this was another "merciless killing of a black man by law enforcement" and set cars on fire, destroyed businesses, smashed windows, defied a curfew, and clashed with officers. By the time authorities restored control, two people died and another was wounded. Four and a half months later, the Kenosha County District Attorney announced, "It is my decision now that no Kenosha law enforcement officer will be charged with any criminal offense based on the facts and laws," The DA went on to report that Blake himself said he had a knife during the incident.

Of the many millions of encounters between law enforcement officers and the public, about a thousand a year result in police killing a suspect. Nationally, many of these go unnoticed, but a handful rocket to the forefront and generate national discussion (a good consequence) as well as riots, looting, and violence (very bad). These killings are invariably the intersection of criminality and confrontation with a cop, a very small number of whom exercise poor judgment.

Leaders can reduce the presence of bad cops and questionable judgments through rigorous recruiting standards, top notch entry-level and recurrent training, high-quality management, and seasoned leadership. Mayors are responsible for selecting law enforcement leaders who know how to implement and oversee such activities to protect both the public and their officers.

Mayors and Governors are also responsible for periodically monitoring law enforcement at department level. Do we regularly and publicly support law enforcement and promote a one-community culture that respects the officers who take an oath to protect and serve? Is our community confident or fearful of our police? Importantly, leaders should insist on department certification by the Commission on Accreditation for Law Enforcement Agencies (CALEA). Of some 18,700 nationwide departments, only 726 are so certified, and 236 are certified with Excellence (including my city's police department, which was initially certified in 1992).

If they sense widespread problems, responsible public leaders invite an outside state or federal department to dig deeper. Following a high-profile police killing in Ferguson, MO, the U.S. Department of Justice investigated that city's police department. A key finding was that "Ferguson's law enforcement practices are shaped by the City's focus on revenue rather than by public safety needs." The DOJ detailed very significant unlawful and racist polices that city leadership either failed to see, involve itself in, or correct.[127]

Obviously, government responsibilities are beyond the control of suspects, so what can *they* do? They alone control their conduct prior to and during an encounter with police. Tragically, just about 100% of them choose criminal conduct. That alone doesn't justify police killing them, but it is a very significant factor that resulted in lethal outcomes that suspects could have prevented.

Here're eleven cases that made national headlines and resulted in significant public furor, violence, and destruction.

Trayvon Martin, Feb 26, 2012, Sanford, FL.
This 17-year old black male was mortally shot by 28-year old George Zimmerman (German-Peruvian) during an altercation in a gated townhouse community parking lot that had recently experienced break-ins and burglaries. Zimmerman was a neighborhood-watch volunteer who observed Martin on a rainy night; he alerted police by cellphone and left his vehicle. The police told Zimmerman to return to his vehicle and he was recorded saying "OK".

Trayvon Martin was no stranger to fighting, drugs, truancy, vandalism (surveillance video shows him defacing school property), and school suspension.[128] That night he was returning from a convenience store to the home of his father's fiancée.

Zimmerman testified that he and Martin exchanged a few words and an altercation ensued. Zimmerman sustained a broken nose and cuts on the back of his head, which he said Martin inflicted by repeatedly slamming his head against the pavement.

Originally not charged (for defending himself), public attention rose to a fever pitch. Rather than calm the nation and call for the justice system to carefully and accurately oversee the path forward, President Barack Obama famously said, "If I had a son, he'd look like Trayvon." Mr. President, your son may have *looked* like Trayvon, but I hope you wouldn't have raised one to *behave* like Trayvon. In a subsequent trial for second-degree murder and manslaughter, the six-woman jury acquitted Zimmerman. That verdict spawned the Black Lives Matter movement (see Chapter 11).

Zimmerman subsequently filed a $100m lawsuit against the Martin family, their lawyer, and others for conspiracy. Records show Trayvon talking by cellphone to his girlfriend just prior to the encounter. His suit contends that the girlfriend didn't want to testify at the murder trial, so her half-sister appeared as the key witness at the trial to testify that *she* heard Zimmerman make prejudicial remarks over the phone to Trayvon.

The case has not gone to trial yet.

Michael Brown Jr. Aug 9, 2014, Ferguson, MO. Race baiters and the ever-compliant media instantly dubbed this incident of "white policeman killing an unarmed black teen" as a cause célèbre. Liberal elected leaders, black athletes, and the Hollywood illuminati tripped over themselves jumping on the bandwagon. Broadcast and print media lackeys descended on the city and spewed the most inflammatory images and narratives they could concoct with cameras and salivate into microphones.

This was a liberal's macabre nirvana. And why shouldn't it be? Since Trevon Martin's death two years earlier, weren't the liberals and media bombarding the public with the idea that police were wantonly killing unarmed black Americans in the streets? "Who *was* the Ferguson bigot with a badge, and why wasn't he already in a cell with murder charges hanging over him?" "No black person is safe in Ferguson or, for that matter, in America!" "Just the latest tragic example of national racism!" "Join the cause, buy our newspapers and subscribe to online feeds! Vote Democrat to erase this lingering lethal legacy of slavery and white privilege!"

The sweeping narrative of massive police shootings of innocent, unarmed Blacks had found a martyr that the NAACP, Jesse Jackson and his Rainbow Push Coalition, Al Sharpton's National

Urban League, civilian and political leaders could ride to notoriety. And sure enough, riots instantly ensued in Ferguson and across the country, burning both white and black businesses. All that was missing were extended warranties for the looted televisions.

A barrage of reporters gladly stuck with and promoted that narrative, stressing that their esteemed 18-year-old saint was an all-around great young man and unarmed when shot.

Notes: "Unarmed" is a reporter's popular adjective to convey benign, much less-threatening situations, one readers picture as a compliant, defenseless youth trembling before a menacing, overbearing, gun-wielding, racist policeman.

In fact, unarmed doesn't mean incapable of inflicting death or great bodily harm. Threatened officers have to immediately consider the subject's prior record (if known), size, prior actions, current demeanor, activity, and intent, as well as every readily available opportunity to quickly acquire and use a weapon - the officer's own pistol, taser, a rock, pipe, you name it.

An officer can draw, aim, and fire his pistol in about 1.5 seconds - the same very brief time it takes an assailant to close on the officer from 21' away.

The liberal media's national coverage consistently presented the victim in the most positive light possible, routinely displaying a high school yearbook picture showing him neatly dressed, well-groomed, and pensive. Seldom if ever does the media cover any criminal record the deceased may have, adverse personal facts, or aspects of the incident that don't support their narrative. Fawning media jumped on the sympathetic term "gentle giant" to describe the imposing 6'4" 295-pound thug (officer Wilson was the same height but 80 lbs. lighter that Brown).

The senior investigating agency was President Obama's U.S. Department of Justice under black Attorney General Eric Holder. Here's a summary of events from their official 86-page memorandum of the incident.

Surveillance video and witness testimony reveal that Michael Brown blatantly stole a handful of cigarillos from a convenience store, assaulted the 5'6" 150-lb clerk who tried to stop him from leaving without paying, and walked down the middle of Canfield Drive with friend Dorian Johnson. The clerk's daughter immediately notified the police, who broadcast the incident.

Nearby Officer Darren Wilson saw Brown and his friend walking in the middle of Canfield Avenue, disrupting traffic. He drove past them to block their path and noticed the cigarillos from the police dispatch a few minutes ago. Wilson parked at an angle in the street to block them and attempted to get out of his police SUV, but was unable to do so as his door rebounded off Brown or Brown pushed it closed.

After cursing Wilson, Brown leaned into the SUV and began assaulting the seated officer. Unable to access less-lethal weapons, Wilson withdrew his gun, which Brown then grabbed and the two struggled to control it.

Wilson fired his pistol, the bullet striking Brown's hand and lodging in the vehicle door. A wounded Brown again leaned into the SUV and assaulted Wilson once more. After Wilson fired a second shot, Brown began running away. Knowing that anyone who would assault a store clerk and an armed officer posed a danger to others, Wilson got out of his SUV and pursued Brown while repeatedly directing him to stop and get on the ground.

Rather than comply, Brown turned around and ran toward Wilson. Wilson feared for his life, backed up, and again repeatedly ordered Brown to stop and get on the ground. Brown again did not comply and charged Wilson. Wilson backed up and fired again. Brown paused once more, then charged a third time Wilson fired additional shots as Brown leaned forward as though he was getting ready to tackle Wilson. Wilson fired a last shot that killed Brown from 8'-10' away.

Brown's accomplice, Dorian Johnson, told investigators that Brown stopped on command, raised his hands in surrender, and verbally urged Wilson, "Don't shoot." Johnson also said Wilson shot Brown in the back.

After interviewing numerous other witnesses, examining physical, forensic, ballistic, crime scene, autopsy, and video evidence, the DOJ came to a concise conclusion that "… this matter lacks prosecutive merit and should be closed."[129]

Never dissuaded by facts and always pitching to the uninformed, two far-left presidential candidates re-stoked racism on the 5th anniversary of the incident with completely baseless and racially polarizing tweets. [130]

Elizabeth Warren ✔
@ewarren

5 years ago Michael Brown was murdered by a white police officer in Ferguson, Missouri. Michael was unarmed yet he was shot 6 times. I stand with activists and organizers who continue the fight for justice for Michael. We must confront systemic racism and police violence head on.

2:59 PM · Aug 9, 2019   ⓘ

♡ 36.1K   ♢ 33.8K people are Tweeting about this

Kamala Harris ✔
@KamalaHarris

Michael Brown's murder forever changed Ferguson and America. His tragic death sparked a desperately needed conversation and a nationwide movement. We must fight for stronger accountability and racial equity in our justice system.

2:24 PM · Aug 9, 2019   ⓘ

♡ 2.9K   ♢ 7.3K people are Tweeting about this

Senator Warren is a former Harvard law professor and Senator Harris, who served seven years as San Francisco's District Attorney and eight years as California's Attorney General, certainly know that officer Wilson did not murder Michael Brown.

Both were wrong but never in doubt. But hey, the hell with educating the public with truth to unify rather than divide the country. "I'm a liberal candidate, so I'm prepared to pull out all the ethical and moral stops to get elected."

Even a cursory look at the facts reveals how the premise of the entire liberal narrative was a complete and utter lie; "journalists" again used the pretext of news to advance a political agenda and grab ratings. Their thrust was that a (presumably racist) white policeman gunned down (in a presumably depravedly manner) an unarmed (presumably peaceful and innocent) black teenager.

The idea of addressing actual instances of police brutality have become diluted by highly-partisan reporting, riots, pillaging, and ignoring the much greater number of annual black-on-black murders (in 2018 the FBI reported Whites killed 234 Blacks, Blacks killed 2,600 Blacks!).[131]

Walter Scott, Apr 4, 2015, North Charleston, SC.
Officer Michael Slager stopped Scott for a malfunctioning brake light. Scott exited his vehicle and began to flee as Slager fatally shot him multiple times in the back. Slager was justifiably arrested, tried, and sentenced to 20 years in prison.

Freddie Gray, Apr 12, 2015, Baltimore, MD.
Gray fled upon seeing two officers on bicycle patrol in a high crime area, causing officers to chase Gray, who had frequent encounters for drug offenses. Police caught and arrested him for possession of an illegal spring-assisted, one-hand operated knife clipped to his pants pocket.[132]

Officers cuffed Gray and loaded him into the rear compartment of a police van. The unrestrained Gray suffered spinal injuries during transport, went into a coma and died a week later. Following its investigations, the U.S. Department Of Justice did not file any charges. The liberal black city attorney filed multiple charges against six officers, which were subsequently dropped or resulted in mistrials and acquittals.

Alton Sterling, 12:30 a.m. July 5, 2016, Baton Rouge, LA.
An individual reported to police that he'd been threatened with a gun by a black man selling CDs on the sidewalk. Officers responded and within 90 seconds they engaged Sterling, attempted to arrest the resisting suspect ("he was very large and very strong"), tasered him,

wrestled him on the ground, saw his right hand go for a pocket, shot him, told Sterling again not to move, saw Sterling again reach into his pocket, saw a gun, and fired three additional bullets. All in a minute and a half. There were no prior incidents involving substantiated allegations of misconduct against the two officers.[133]

Botham Jean, Sep 6, 2018, Dallas, TX.
Off-duty Dallas Police Dept. patrol officer Amber Guyger entered the Dallas, TX apartment of 26-year-old accountant Botham Jean and fatally shot him. Guyger said that she believed it was her apartment and shot Jean in the belief he was a burglar. The fact that Guyger, a white police officer, shot and killed Jean, an unarmed black man, and was initially only charged with manslaughter, resulted in protests and accusations of racial bias. On October 1, 2019, Guyger was found guilty of murder. The next day, she received a sentence of ten years in prison.

Atatiana Jefferson, Oct 12, 2019, Ft. Worth, TX.
A neighbor called police very early in the morning to investigate Atatiana's open front door. As officers walked around the house in the dark, Atatiana heard a noise, pulled a gun from her purse, and pointed it at the window. Officer Aaron Dean yelled "Put your hands up! Show me your hands!" before firing through the window and killing her. Neither officer identified themselves as police. On December 20, 2019, a grand jury indicted Dean for murder. The case remains open and active.

Ahmaud Arbery, Feb 23, 2020 Brunswick, GA
Three white civilians pursued, shot, and killed Arbery in their neighborhood, saying they wanted to question him about recent thefts from houses under construction. Following initial decisions not to prosecute and a DA's recusal, the Georgia Bureau of Investigation arrested all three on counts of felony murder in May, 2020. The Georgia Attorney General also requested FBI intervention, which was granted. The case remains open and active.

Breona Taylor, Mar 13, 2020, Louisville, KY.

I've Had Enough!

An internal Louisville Metro Police report and corroborating evidence showed that Breona Taylor had extensive ties with a suspected drug trafficker in a large narcotics investigation. Three plainclothes Louisville Metro Police officers were serving a no-knock warrant at her apartment. Per a witness, they announced themselves two times, then forced the door open. Breona's boyfriend opened fire and hit an officer. Breona died from return fire.[134]

In May, 2020, KY Commonwealth Attorney Tom Wine recommended that Judge Olu Stevens dismiss attempted homicide of a police officer charges against boyfriend Kenneth Walker pending independent investigations by the KY AG's Office, the FBI, and the U.S. Attorney's Office. KY is reviewing its policy on no-knock warrants and use of bodycams by plainclothes officers.

In Sep, 2020 a grand jury indicted one of the officers on three counts of wanton endangerment.

George Floyd, May 25, 2020, Minneapolis, MN.
Minneapolis police approached Floyd in his vehicle after a complaint that he'd used a counterfeit $20 to buy merchandise. Responding officer Lane reports Floyd resisted attempts to be handcuffed but became compliant when moved to a sidewalk, then sat there and conversed for two minutes.

Officers Lane and Kueng then walked 6' 6" 240-lb Floyd to a squad car. Floyd told them he was claustrophobic and resisted efforts to get him inside. Floyd said he couldn't breathe and an officer removed him through the rear passenger-side door. Officers kept him on the ground as he moved back and forth. One officer continued using his knee to pin Floyd's neck for almost 3 minutes after Floyd became unresponsive.

Emergency medical personnel arrived several minutes later and transported Floyd to the Hennepin County Medical Center where he was pronounced dead. Separate autopsies reached different conclusions regarding Floyd's cause of death. "The [Hennepin County Medical Examiner's] autopsy revealed no physical findings that support a diagnosis of traumatic asphyxia or strangulation. Mr. Floyd had underlying health conditions including coronary artery disease and hypertensive heart disease."[135]

Hennepin County Medical Examiner Dr. Andrew Baker later reported that Floyd had 11 ng/mL of fentanyl in his system and told investigators, "If he were found dead at home alone and no other apparent causes, this could be acceptable to call an OD. Deaths have been certified with levels of 3." [136]

An independent autopsy stated that compression [from the officer's knee on Floyd's neck] cut off blood to his brain, and weight on his back made it hard to breathe.

The officers have been arrested and are awaiting trial.

Rayshard Brooks, June 12, 2020., Atlanta, GA. [137]

Accepting a plea deal for several 2014 offenses, 27-year old Rayshard Brooks served a year in prison and was on probation in 2020. Responding to a complaint in June 2020, police found Rayshard asleep at the wheel of his car, blocking a Wendy's restaurant drive-through lane. They administered a field sobriety test that showed Brooks had a blood-alcohol level of .108% - 13x the legal limit of .08%.

As the two officers attempted to arrest Brooks, video shows he very aggressively resisted, wrestled both of them to the ground, stole officer Rolfs' taser, and fled on foot. When officer Rolfs pursued him, Brooks turned and shot the taser at Rolfs. Atlanta police are equipped with tasers having two cartridges, so Brooks still had the capability to tase Rolfs, take his firearm, and use it to commit another crime. Officer Rolfs returned fire and Brooks died shortly thereafter at the hospital.

Brooks would very likely have been remanded back to prison if he'd been arrested, which may have motivated his violent resistance. [138]

Black Democrat Mayor Keisha Bottoms fired Rolfs immediately and black Fulton County District Attorney Paul Howard (running for reelection) promptly charged both officers: Rolfs with felony murder and ten other offenses; Brosnan with aggravated assault and two counts of violation of oath. Their trials are pending. Paul Howard lost reelection, receiving only 27% of votes cast.

I've Had Enough!

Two other notable cases that did *not* result in a police shooting involved Henry Louis Gates Jr. and Jussie Smollett.

On July 16, 2009, Cambridge, MA Police Sgt. James Crowley responded to a possible housebreaking by two black males. At the scene, he saw an older black male in the foyer and asked if he would step outside. The male, later identified as Professor Henry Gates, replied, "No, I will not." While Officer Crowley identified himself and explained why he was there, Gates said "Why, because I'm a black man in America?" [139]

Concerned if housebreakers or an accomplice were in the house, Officer Crowley asked Gates if anyone else was inside. Gates began yelling at Crowley, told him it was none of his business, told Crowley he had no idea who he was messing with, and accused Crowley of being a racist police officer.

Sgt. Crowley asked for a photo ID to confirm that Gates was the rightful occupant of the house; Gates initially refused, followed Crowley onto the porch yelling and accusing Crowley of racial bias. Crowley warned Gates that he was becoming disorderly, which Gates ignored and persisted. Sgt. Crowley arrested Gates for disorderly conduct.

Gates was detained for four hours and the charges were dropped within five days. The week after the incident, President Obama said "… the Cambridge Police Department acted stupidly…" and later invited both men to the White House to sit down over a beer. Both have met on other occasions and Crowley gave Gates the handcuffs used during the arrest (which Gates donated to the Smithsonian National Museum of African American History and Culture).

Gates' use of Chris Rock's rules #2 and #5, and #6 instead of acting on his racial bias would have prevented the escalation. After confirming Gates as the occupant of the house, Sgt. Crowley had the option of enduring some verbal abuse and leaving the scene.

In another highly publicized case, 38-year-old gay black actor **Jussie Smollett** reported to Chicago police that he'd been assaulted by two masked racist, anti-gay men outside his apartment at 2:00 AM on January 29, 2019. Per Smollett, the attackers battered him about the face, yelled "Make America Great Again", doused him with a chemical, and placed a rope around his neck - which he was still wearing when the police arrived at his apartment some 45 minutes later.

Since the supposed victim was black, gay, and an actor, the media quickly ran the story as front-page news. Kamala Harris, then a Democrat presidential candidate, jumped at the chance for publicity by irresponsibly calling the incident a "modern-day lynching." Certainly not the kind of thoughtful restraint we need in a senior public official.

Upon investigation, however, Chicago investigators discovered substantial evidence of Smollett having orchestrated the entire episode for notoriety that would lead to higher pay and promote his career. He paid Nigerian brothers Abimbola and Olabinjo Osundairo $3,500 to participate as the assailants. Additional investigation found store surveillance video of the two Nigerians purchasing the rope that Smollett used in the fabricated attack.

In March, 2019, the Cook County, IL State's Attorney's Office charged the actor with feloniously making false reports to the Chicago Police. Later in the month, however, black State's Attorney Kim Foxx dropped all charges with the thin rationalization that Smollett had forfeited his $10k bond to the government and served 16 hours of community service.

Following widespread outrage as mentioned earlier in Chapter 9, Judge Michael Toomin appointed a special investigator to reexamine the case. A Cook County, IL grand jury approved six new criminal charges and Smollett could also be assessed the costs of investigations. As of this writing, the state has not set a trial date. The unfortunate consequence of the matter is how Smollett and Foxx have lowered the credibility of true racial bias cases in the public's mind.

Take-Away

Progressives reflexively and habitually cry "Wolf!" every time they ordain martyrs of active felons committing yet another violent crime, defying instructions that would de-escalate the situation, forcibly resisting arrest, attacking officers, and ultimately getting shot in the process. When the truth surrounding their

I've Had Enough!

incomplete, misleading, or downright fallacious storylines emerges, any former sympathies evaporate. The very dangerous consequence is a lack of support for actual cases of police

Chapter 13: Serve and Protect

"Do you know why I pulled you over?" Like most American drivers, the police have probably asked you that question at least once (hopefully resulting in just a warning).

The U.S. Department of Justice estimated 53 *million* police contacts with people aged 16 or older in 2015.[140] Just under a thousand of those, 994, ended up with police killing a suspect. In 732 of those fatal incidents, suspects attacked officers or others and they were significant threats in 218 other cases. The Washington Post Fatal Force data base lists the threat status in the remaining 43 cases as undetermined.[141]

While the stakes in these intensely stressful, split-second events are of the highest order, painfully few entities have a record of only one dire outcome in every 53,000 situations (U.S. airlines do very well with their 16m annual flights and are way ahead of fatal medical errors). As good as law enforcement performance is, how can we improve it?

Liberals listened to proposals at their August 2020 Democrat National Convention. There, a featured a panelist who's Wake Forest bio identified her as a "nonbinary/gender transcendent mermaid Queen-King" called for the abolition of the police, U.S. Immigration and Customs Enforcement (ICE), and prisons. She naively asked, "Why can't folks imagine a world without the cops? Why can't folks imagine a world without prisons? Why can't people expand their imaginations to include community care, to include an abolitionist future?" J Mai stressed that she was talking about *real* abolition, not a watered-down version. "We're talking about abolishing the police, we're talking about abolishing ICE, we're talking about abolishing prisons."

The realistic path to reducing the number of prisoners is raising people who don't become criminals – which takes significantly more thought and effort that simply wishing prisons away. It's difficult to know whether it's more alarming for a major political party to feature her at a convention workshop, or that a roomful of delegates actually listened to her. Are these productive paths forward? Do they even *remotely* consider the realities of human nature?

Effective departments that earn public trust for truly policing a community's well-being have the full and reliable support of their elected bosses: governors, state legislators, county commissioners, mayors, and city councils. Those officials have to engage with senior law enforcers to understand their needs for policies and resources and regularly support them in public forums. They don't always get it right.

Following several high-profile cases, elected officials, public figures, and the media invariably issued premature, inflammatory statements and opinions before learning fundamental truths (such as the previously-covered MN Governor immediately after Jacob Blake's shooting). They spoke very publicly without knowing critical facts about the circumstances or subject, his record, any accomplices, on-site officers' conduct, and crowds. Their rash statements (such as "Police *murdered* another unarmed black man!") created, broadened, and intensified hysteria that resulted in public outrage, demonstrations, looting, property destruction, and additional injuries and deaths.

Liberal mayors did not stand with their police chiefs and reassure the public that they were confident in the overall department, would launch an immediate, transparent, and through investigation, and place the involved officers on administrative leave pending its outcome. They would enforce the law across the board. If they weren't confident enough in their departments to support them, they were grossly negligent in making those departments worthy of such confidence.

The 2020 Minneapolis City Council has been one of the most outspoken police critics in the country. Council President Lisa Bender raised eyebrows with her June, 2020 comments during an interview on CNN. She said that calling the police when your home is broken into "comes from a place of privilege." No, Lisa, not from a place of privilege, but from a moral society with a culture of order, respect for the law, government priority on safety, responsible elected officials, and public support.

Immediately after officer Garrett Rolf shot parolee Rayshard Brooks in Atlanta, Mayor Keisha Bottoms fired him without so much as a preliminary investigation. She went on to spew the obligatory lament, "That could have been any one of us, that could be any of our kids or brothers." Could it? Only if they had a history of crime, incarceration, driving under the influence at the time of the incident, fighting two officers to the ground, stealing their taser and firing it at the officer while fleeing. Other than that, Mayor, I guess there's no difference at all. Rather than support the Atlanta Police Department, Mayor Bottoms also accepted Police Chief Erika Shields' resignation less than 24 hours after the shooting. Six months later the police reported a 53% year-to-date increase in murders and auto thefts rose 45% in the preceding 28-day period.[142]

Elected leadership's failure to enforce the law when demonstrations bend towards violence sends the clear message to far-left and anarchist lawbreakers that leaders will tolerate further mayhem. Then others, who were taking a wait-and-see approach before venting their life's frustrations, join the fray, along with more hardened criminals who see opportunities to loot, rob, and pillage. By that time, officials have ripped the lid off Pandora's box and face an increasingly difficult task of restoring the culture of civilized conduct.

Rebecca Pringle, current president of the nation's largest labor union (with 3+m members) is a spokesmodel for far-left socialist doctrine. As president of the National Education Association (NEA) she blatantly endorses an in-vogue Marxist organization and trash-talks law enforcement in her opening message of the NEA Policy Playbook, "… our consciousness has been rocked by images of unarmed black men and women being murdered by those who had vowed to protect them - and with no accountability." [143] Given that the vast majority of the union members are government teachers, one can only wonder how broadly her poisonous lies are being spread to developing minds.

Liberals promoting their narrative of unbridled police violence against Blacks are duping listeners, seeding unrest, and completely missing how so much of the population has become numb to the repetitious screaming rants of "police brutality" - if they ever listened in the first place. "There go the crazy libs again, with no clue what they're talking about, and throwing down the worn-out, dog-eared race card instead of practical, effective policy ideas. Maybe the transcendent mermaid Queen-King can help them out."

Fair, effective, community-oriented law enforcement never "just happens", it's developed by everyone concerned, including citizens. Yes, individuals are also responsible for knowing how politicians vote on issues, and occasionally calling officials or their staffs to learn about performance.

As shown in Chapter 11, some officers clearly and feloniously exercised lethal force. Some were also the subject of multiple complaints. This begs the question, "Why don't departments have better officers?"

Great people make great cops, and that begins with recruiting. All quality departments review their accession standards and procedures to accept only those who meet them and showing the door to those who don't. Law enforcement departments routinely experience line officer shortages due to too few fully-qualified applicants, especially with minorities. Seattle has seen their applicant numbers drop 90% since 2008; Boston has a pool of only 56 candidates to fill 458 projected retirements.[144] After all, the hours are long, they may be spent in dangerous situations, and mayors in cities like Seattle, Portland, Los Angeles, Minneapolis, Atlanta, and New York have thrown officers, police chiefs, and whole departments under the bus in a second. Would you encourage *your* kids to join under those conditions?

Effective recruit training is relevant, performance-based, and continuous. How thoroughly does it include proper arrest and restraint procedures? Incident de-escalation? How relevant is the training to intensive, fast-breaking scenarios that cadets will encounter in the field? Who evaluates the instructors and material for self-taught classes? Is it properly certified?

Good departments also monitor performance in the field and review complaints to determine when an officer needs additional training or supervision, discipline, or termination. Successful departments promptly recognize and publicize facts regarding violent incidents involving their officers. Do the department and the District Attorney root out and prosecute bad cops?

Elected officials and their departments achieve long-term public support when they promote officers' essential role to maintain a civilized, safe community, encourage competent citizens to join, and showcase accomplishments.[145]

Augmenting police with separate specialists to handle non-violent issues is under consideration in a growing number of departments. St. Petersburg, FL Mayor Rick Kriseman and Police Chief Anthony Holloway jointly introduced such a program in July, 2020 whereby police would no longer respond to non-violent situations.[146] Continued or enhanced police/social worker presence in high-density residential and minority-owned business areas may be impossible where inner cities run by liberals denigrate and work to defund law enforcement.

One group studying police use-of-force policies reports that adherence to eight measures significantly reduces the number of police killings. They go on to say that few departments have adopted them; CALEA-certified departments have, has yours?

% Fewer Police Dept. Killings With Each Policy Implemented

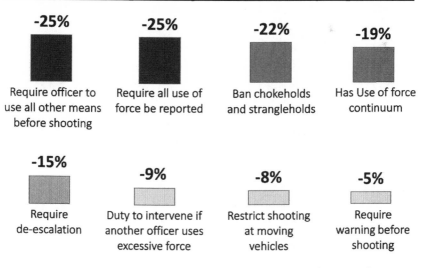

| -25% | -25% | -22% | -19% |
| Require officer to use all other means before shooting | Require all use of force be reported | Ban chokeholds and strangleholds | Has Use of force continuum |

| -15% | -9% | -8% | -5% |
| Require de-escalation | Duty to intervene if another officer uses excessive force | Restrict shooting at moving vehicles | Require warning before shooting |

Source: UseOfForceProject.org

I've Had Enough!

How're your district attorney and judges doing? Have you ever inquired about the sentencing for similar crimes and criminal histories along racial lines? How long is the trial backlog?

The single most significant factor in reducing lethal encounters with police are the *suspects themselves*. Several years ago, black comedian Chris Rock presented a skit called "How To Not Get Your Ass Kicked By The Police". While a bit tongue-in-cheek, following Chris' rules would have prevented *nearly every one* of the high-profile cases that made headlines and hundreds of others that haven't. Here they are:

- Obey the law [this is the most obvious tip, yet most victims were indeed committing a crime - many of them violent]
- Use common sense
- Stop immediately if you're directed to do so
- Turn that sh*t off [stop playing music loudly while cruising or stopped by the police]
- Be polite
- Shut the f**k up [when stopped, don't intensify the situation by screaming and swearing]
- Get a white friend [instead of giving a ride to a Black who has weapons, drugs, or outstanding warrants]
- Don't ride with a mad woman [she'll tell the police anything just so they'll kick your ass!]

Chapter 14: Who Matters

T he *Black Lives Matter* organization and message gained significant momentum from the distorted media spin surrounding the Ferguson, MO shooting. The emotional slogan has become a rallying cry for anyone with any real or imagined gripe about society or frustrations with some aspects of their personal life.

The catchy title garnered a national following that promoted the fearful notion that police throughout the country were wantonly murdering innocent black people whenever and wherever they found them. It became a rallying cry, yet very few devotees looked into the highly distorted narrative of rampant police brutality they heard and assumed was true.

There's a distinct difference between the obvious moral statement that black lives matter, and the activist political organization itself. The obvious moral statement that black people's lives matter is a glaringly obvious reality, and no more profound than saying the earth is round. With very few exceptions, it's universally accepted.

The organization, though, is something different, much different. Activists Alicia Garza, Patrice Cullors, and Opal Tometi started the BLM movement in 2013 following George Zimmerman's acquittal for defending himself from Trayvon Martin.

Apparently, the three founders didn't wait to learn the truth about the incident: President Obama's Department of Justice concluded there was insufficient evidence to prosecute Zimmerman on either hate crimes or civil rights charges.[147] In Florida, a full jury acquitted him of 2nd degree murder or manslaughter. Maybe, though, the founders were all *too aware* of the facts and chose to ignore them. Either way, they've had mainstream media's adoring support the whole way.

Co-founder Patrisse Cullors stated in a 2015 video that she and fellow organizers were "trained Marxists" and schooled under the Labor/Community Strategy Center by its director, Eric Mann – early leader of the Weather Underground and convicted of conspiracy to commit murder.[148]

I've Had Enough!

Toronto BLM co-founder Yusra Khogali tweeted "Plz Allah give me strength to cuss/kill these men and white folks out here today. Plz plz plz".[149]

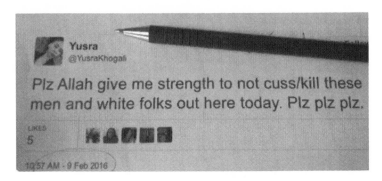

Yusra
@YusraKhogali

Plz Allah give me strength to not cuss/kill these men and white folks out here today. Plz plz plz.

LIKES
5

10:57 AM - 9 Feb 2016

Ariel Atkins, BLM activist in Chicago, widely voiced her perspective on looting there, "I don't care if someone decides to loot, because that makes sure that person eats or has clothes. Anything they want to take, they can, because these businesses have insurance." What? Does she think they're going to eat Nike shoes, or sell them for grocery money? To her credit, Mayor Lightfoot brought the city's rioters under control much more rapidly than her counterparts in Portland and Seattle.

London saw armed robberies explode from 12 in 1954, when anyone could buy a shotgun, to 1,600 in 1991 when there were increasingly severe restrictions on firearms sales. There's no evidence that there was more poverty there in the second half of that century than the first. What has changed is attitudes towards law and order.[150]

The Armed Conflict Location and Event Data Project (ACLED) reported about 570 violent demonstrations in 2020, with well over 80% connected to Black Lives Matter movement or the COVID-19 pandemic.[151] Such actions do nothing to reduce discrimination, but much to perpetuate and intensify stereotypes of black lawlessness.

Such is the basis of the Black Lives Matter organization. Today, its sympathizers range from those who are sincerely concerned for equality and justice, to frustrated indulged liberal punks, hoodlums, and anarchists. Unfortunately, any real concerns, messages, and progress are lost in news videos of rampant lawlessness. BLM is increasingly associated with Burn, Loot, and Murder.

As of this writing, you can visit the BLM website (it's a .com, for commercial, instead of a .org for organization), where clicking the "donate" button takes you directly to actblu.com [Act Blue]– a technology organization that raises money for left-leaning causes.

I've Had Enough!

Chapter 15: White Privilege or Black Burden?

W hy does a greater proportion of some races have more wealth, security, and a higher standard of living than others?

Whenever disparities arise, liberals automatically identify them along racial lines and instinctively conclude that "White privilege" is the culprit. Even when power or other attributes (financial or personal effort, for example) are at the root of a disparity and there's merely a correlation with race, liberals brand every white person with the scarlet letters 'WP'.

Liberals repeatedly name-call with the defective, demeaning, one-size-fits-all slur. They use it regardless of whether members of the targeted demographic pulled themselves up through an enlistment in the military or years on an assembly line, haven't inherited any wealth from relatives, or are poverty-stricken white residents of Eastern Kentucky: every White is privileged because of skin color. What could be more racist?

To any number of Whites, the term is a pejorative, divisive, political campaign epithet used by racist liberals to demonize others and attract supporters. In this regard, all Whites are the left's immoral boogeymen whose entire history has left the world in ruin. Score extra points when you can work in additional adjectives such as "old", "male", and "European" - making the speaker guilty of ageism, sexism, and xenophobia. One wonders why they don't talk about Asian Privilege accounting for *that* race's success.

An online video intends to vividly illustrate how "white privilege" works. It begins with a line of multi-racial high school students on a field where an adult places a $100 bill on the ground some distance ahead of them. The adult challenges the kids to race for it, "But first", he says, "I'm going to make a few statements, and if they apply to you, take two steps forward."

"Take two steps forward if both of your parents are still married." A number of students step forward; notably, some black ones do not.

I've Had Enough!

"Take two steps forward if you grew up with a father figure in the home." Again, the camera features several black students who remain on the original line.

"Take two steps forward if you had access to a private education. Take two steps forward if you never had to help mom or dad with the bills." Same results as before.

"Every statement I've made has nothing to do with anything any of you have done, has nothing to do with decisions you've made." Maybe the coach overlooked any of the white students' attendance, homework, and study habits, or their decisions to avoid crime and avoid parental indebtedness for attorneys, fines, and a record that would inhibit their future.

"We don't want to recognize that we've been given a head start, but the reality is we have." Isn't that what families do?

When the students finally race ahead, one of the white contenders captures the prize, as expected.

In liberal minds, this proves that Whites get ahead strictly due to privileges owing to their skin color. Very emotional, very graphic, very politicized, and very inaccurate. How would the event unfold if the coach asked questions about attributes like artistic or athletic abilities: "Take two steps forward if you made the basketball or football team? Take two steps forward if you received any scholarship money for any of your abilities?"

It clearly ignores the benefits of generational adherence to successful behaviors and the compiling negative effects of other choices.

While watching the clip, I heard and saw two predominant messages: those who end up ahead of the original line are only there due to their race, and everyone else is preordained to a 3rd-rate future with no recourse, options, or opportunities for the next 65 years of their lives because they don't enjoy "white privilege".

Both of those messages neglect key life lessons for developing one's potential for a better future. The USA offers more self-improvement chances than any other society throughout recorded history. Being comprised of people, it won't achieve perfection, but it's the best there is and that's a major privilege we *all* enjoy.

R.J. Ross

> **On a personal Note**: Other privileges I enjoy
>
> - Parents who loved, cared for, and raised me
> - Teachers and study habits that prepared me for college
> - The sense to avoid criminal behavior, drugs, and immoderate use of alcohol
> - A college ROTC program and Army officer commission
> - Great Army bosses, recognition of my duty performance, and selections for promotions, assignments, and additional schooling
> - Federally-authorized Roth IRA and America's positive market impacts on investments in it

As world champion professional boxer Muhammad Ali said after his title fight in Zaire, Africa, "I'm glad my great grandpa got on that boat."[152]

Given the initial differences in the racers' starting points, the real question becomes, "What factors enabled some families to provide a better start for their kids and hindered others from doing so?" Is *race* the cause of the differences, or is race a correlative factor? The video doesn't give us sufficient information about the individuals or their families to answer that. Liberals, though, will be quick to unquestionably conclude that the difference is due to... racism.

Focusing on other people's lives, incomes, and cell phones creates an envy/victimology mentality that does nothing to advance yourself. Worse, it deflects attention from what you *can* change - using your own abilities, potential, and choices to improve yourself and the lives of your children - or your personal decision not to.

Now back to the demonstration. The premise of this and a thousand other liberal arguments is that lives start and are confined to one line, and all Whites enjoy inherent privileges guaranteeing them a win. With that defective premise firmly established in their minds, the natural next step is for white people to make everyone's outcomes equal through direct and indirect payments, promotions, and admissions. This particular demonstration assumes that the poorest, most neglected and discriminated-against child is the baseline for judging everyone else. That, of course, is clearly a liberal distortion to promote their narrative. Here's a more realistic construct for the instructions in the $100 exercise:

"Throughout nature, parents raise their young until they're self-sufficient; that's what's expected – it's nature's norm, not an exception. If both your parents have been and still are involved in your development, stay where you are, but if one of them *chose* not to be in your life, that *choice* moves you back two steps. If both your parents made the *choice* to exclude you, their *choices* move you back two more steps."

"Certain behaviors significantly and directly impact your future. If you've *chosen* behaviors resulting in unplanned children who you're struggling to care for at the expense of your education or work (or worse, not caring for at all), take another two steps back. Otherwise, stay where you are."

"If you've begun a life of crime, take two steps backwards; another two if it includes violent crimes."

"If you've *chosen* to smoke, use drugs, and drink alcohol, take two steps back, and another two if you've chosen these behaviors to excess."

"Every society requires learned skills to survive, and even more of them to thrive. If you've *chosen* to take full advantage of the 12-year $12,000- $23,000-per-year expense that society's earners pay to educate you, stay put - that's what's expected of you.[153] If, on the other hand, you've *chosen* to only partially apply yourself, take two steps backwards, and another two steps back if you've *chosen* to drop out. "If you've *chosen* to drop out and *chosen* not to earn a GED or complete a skills-development program, take another two steps back from the line."

This focus reveals *actionable causes* of an encumbered behind-the-line starting position much more accurately than those in the video. As a result, "Minority Burden" would be a more accurate term for the relative standing of some minority members.

Another interpretation of White Privilege includes more of a historical origin – beginning with the uncompensated slave labor that enriched early white American slave owners. With that in mind, "White benefit" may be a more apropos term than "White privilege". The most appropriate titles, however, are empowered and powerless, which were the necessary foundations for each party's role in so many past and present situations, incidents, and occurrences.

Liberals continue to define the conflict as between races, ethnicities, and gender. Defining the conflict that way implies, for example, that every Black has been subjugated. Similarly, it implies that all Whites are oppressors. Both those, like the premise, just aren't so.

While race is the current debate in vogue, the abuse of one group of Americans by another certainly hasn't been confined to former white slave owners and former black slaves and their descendants - even after the Emancipation Proclamation. Robber barons Andrew Carnegie (steel), John D. Rockefeller (Standard Oil), Cornelius Vanderbilt (shipping, 1850-60s), and John Pierpont Morgan (railroads, 1885) achieved astounding wealth on the backs of mostly *white* laborers. Yes, their workers were meagerly compensated and weren't the barons' legal property, but the immoral brutality and those workers' hopelessness were akin to that of freedmen's' descendants. If injustices and persecutions were causally paramount, Jews would be some of the poorest and least educated people in the world today.[154]

The simplistic White Male Privilege attention and power-grab campaign slogan is routinely stoked by manipulative race/gender politicians and hucksters; Al Sharpton and Jesse Jackson stand out. They shamelessly promote themselves by shifting blame for constituents' personal conditions to another easily-identifiable group. They'd all make proud Joseph Goebbels, the Nazi Propaganda Minister who tagged non-Aryans as his targeted evil-doers, (see his slickly done one-hour film *Der Ewige Jude* on YouTube).

When dealing with entire populations, there are, of course, exceptions. There're certainly cases of bigoted white, black, Hispanic, Asian, male or female bosses favoring subordinates based strictly on skin color and gender.

But, you say, there *are* a lot of white males in positions of leadership, power, and influence. If the *White Privilege* argument is

I've Had Enough!

bogus, why are so many of them found in ascendant positions? That's a topic for Chapter 15.

Chapter 16: Behaviors

O ver the millennia since the early Chinese, Egyptians, Greeks, Romans, and Germanic tribes to the present, people have developed and adhered to selected behaviors that enabled them to accomplish increasingly complex endeavors. By extension, the more people in a group who practice these behaviors, and do so to a greater extent, the more successful that society becomes ("successful" is defined in the next chapter).

News outlets show mobs of people who are dissatisfied, frustrated, and distressed with their jobs (or lack thereof), their financial status, ideas about society (ala the mermaid Queen/King), some other aspect of their lives, or just matters in general. They don't seem to understand how to survive, excel, and achieve satisfaction in our highly-developed society with all its options. I'm not talking about highly technical knowledge out of college textbooks, but fundamentals of life. In the midst of opportunities all around them, they don't know how to proceed. Like befuddled drivers approaching a busy traffic circle without knowing who has the right-of-way, they don't understand fundamental behavioral "rules of the road". Their primary response, then, is to lash out at our Constitutional form of government and open market economy in hopes of somehow changing their life.

These few behaviors are absolute, not relative to members' feelings and opinions of the day, and have withstood the test of time in a variety of cultures. They also prevail over the latest elites' assurances of superior intellect and ideas that will succeed where human nature has thwarted every such prior attempt.

Notably, the behaviors are neutral in terms of race, gender, ethnicity, faith, and sexual orientation. Liberals may decry them for being too restrictive and some may label them for being "too white". If you're aiming for success, though, doesn't it make sense to learn from successful people of every stripe throughout history and into our current society? And if you *don't* emulate the behaviors of successful people because their race, language, religion, or ethnicity is different than yours, who *do* you emulate? Separate-but-equal and multiculturalism have a poor track record here and abroad.

As with every truly worthwhile achievement, maximum results aren't immediate; living these behaviors is a life style. Let's look at them.

1. Observe a time-proven **moral code** that respects others, particularly the powerless, the young, old, and infirm. Exercise fair practices, even in the face of immoral opportunities to advance monetarily, socially, or professionally. Faith teaches and underpins this behavior for many.

Oppose abuses to others, often perpetrated by overly-ambitious men and women who frequently injure and exploit people through the institution of government. Honor your choices and take ownership of their consequences.

Interestingly, Marxists practice a completely different and contradictory code; morality as we commonly know it is irrelevant. They embrace any action advancing "the workers' struggle against capitalist owners" to achieve the intermediate system of socialism, then full communism. Marx himself wrote,

"Right can never be higher than the economic structure of society and the cultural development thereby determined. We therefore reject every attempt to impose on us any moral dogma whatsoever as an eternal, ultimate and forever immutable moral law."

Scary stuff, but progressives celebrate and fully accept it.

When you don't observe a moral code: You diminish your stature as an individual, and lessen the identity and worth of others.

Senior officers at major banks clearly failed to meet moral standards when they employed predatory lending practices. All too many elected officials don't practice this fundamental behavior either. Ditto for entertainment's writers, producers, directors, and actors who create and glorify immoral and illegal behavior in products they peddle to developing, vulnerable minds.

Judging others as inferior, sometimes to the point of subhuman status and unworthy of any care, consideration, or compassion, ultimately leads to murderous consequences: the Jews in WWII

R.J. Ross

Germany and the Rohingya in Myanmar. Closer to home, consider this mid-1800s description of the Irish in Boston:

"In the popular press, the Irish were depicted as sub-human. They were carriers of disease. They were drawn as lazy, clannish, unclean, drunken brawlers who wallowed in crime and bred like rats."[155]

"It is not because men's desires are strong that they act ill; it is because their consciences are weak."

John Stuart Mill

2. Establish and adhere to a **legal system,** based on laws enacted by chosen representatives, that lays out orderly processes for society's activities. The U.S. Constitution is our most fundamental legal document – the basis for all our derivative laws.

Understand that the role of government is to defend individual rights instead of facilitating equal outcomes, and recognize when it strays from that imperative. Clearly understand that the source of government authority is from the governed, and individuals cannot cede an authority to government they don't have.

Read the U.S. and your state Constitutions and evaluate politicians' adherence to them. Understand the rationale for the three branches of government, their enumerated authorities, and limitations.

Familiarize yourself with issues. No matter how pleasurable or gratifying their appeal, are they Constitutionally authorized, morally sound, and affordable? Know which candidates are on which side of key issues and vote accordingly.

Understand that all the money government disburses it ultimately takes from other families – government is nothing more than a conduit. Business taxes deprive that revenue's use to business owners and investors' 401k and Roth IRA retirement plans. More than 25 million companies are sole proprietors that rely on every dollar to build their business and support their families (less than 1% have receipts of $1m or more).[156]

<u>When you don't</u>: Politicians overstep and abuse their power, use tax money to enrich themselves, and buy votes to stay in power.

I've Had Enough!

Unelected leaders arise to make their own coercive rules instead of those enacted by people's elected representatives acting for the general welfare.

3. Develop and employ **critical thinking.** Expose yourself to alternate and contrarian perspectives so you can better articulate truth-based strengths and flawed arguments. Learn to focus on verifiable facts and their relationship to each other and the overall topic at hand; distance yourself from emotional conclusions and those who rely on and benefit from them. Judge people by their actions more than their words. Seek truth.

When you don't: You and your society are more easily led by dishonest, immoral, and manipulative leaders. You expend more resources, and will support dubious causes when you limit inputs to those from like-minded people's opinions, social media, and late-night comedy shows that are more focused on ratings/profits than truth and perspectives.

4. **Communicate effectively**. Learn and correctly use a common language that effectively conveys thoughts, positions, and ideas generally, as well as intricate matters of science, medicine, governance, business, history, and the humanities. Knowing English opens up enormous worldwide troves of stored knowledge.

When you don't: Limiting knowledge and use to another language excludes full participation in and benefits of our society. Reliance on group slang, with its attendant inability to broadly and effectively communicate to those beyond the group, similarly limits users' chances of personal and professional success.

5. Learn, develop, employ, and improve **skills** to support yourself and your family without becoming a burden to others.

In our complex world we can travel coast-to-coast in four hours while enjoying dinner and wine in a recliner at 35,000'. Sophisticated vehicles are driving themselves; a worldwide virtual store allows millions of buyers and sellers to transact business electronically without ever seeing each other. Fully-equipped emergency vehicles can reach most distressed people in minutes and rapidly move them to medical facilities that're the envy of the world.

The highly diverse society that conceives of, builds, designs, operates, manages, and maintains those and countless other capabilities relies on an extremely broad range of skills. When people don't acquire and employ them, they will only succeed *on the margins or not at all*. America still needs less-skilled manual laborers, but increasingly, it runs on creativity, ever more complex trades, responsive services, information management, and technical expertise.

With a rapidly changing world, people often find their initial skills inadequate or obsolete, and must update their knowledge or pursue entirely new career fields to compete. McDonald's is replacing counter staff with kiosks. Home Depot uses self-checkout stations instead of cashiers. Who will design, build, install, and maintain them? Who heard of Artificial Intelligence (AI) engineers 20 years ago?

Take full advantage of developmental opportunities. If you are a leader in politics, business, faith, community, sports, or entertainment, continually emphasize the criticality of education to students, young adults, and those already in the workforce. You have an increased moral responsibility to underclass whites, inner-city minorities who lack an education culture, and those with an anti-assimilation attitude.

Join a trade or professional association, take on-line courses, read material relevant to your job, or take employer-paid courses classes when they're available. It's a life-long endeavor; you never graduate.

The Launch, Expose, Advise, and Direct (L.E.A.D.) program in Atlanta, GA does a great job in developing black youths through baseball. How about coordinating recurring appearances of local celebrities at inner-city schools to encourage learning?

Maximize what's offered through public education, seek formal and informal opportunities to go further, such as trade schools, internships, scholarships, volunteering, and military service.

When you don't. Individuals as well as societies that don't keep up and adapt eventually become irrelevant. You significantly reduce the chance to sustain yourself and your family and become less competitive for more responsibility, promotions, and their associated compensations.

If higher education is your thing, there's nothing inherently wrong with Art History and Women's Studies, but don't blame open markets or white males if society doesn't reward many of those graduates with related careers and competitive pay.

Those who choose to remain intellectually static are likely to envy others and be mis-led by power-hungry charlatans; they more easily relegate themselves to a lifelong struggle to acquire even the basics, much less enjoy a secure, robust, and fulfilling life.

6. Be **responsible** to yourself, your family, your employer, others, and country. Don't take from others, either directly or via the government, what you can and should earn through your own efforts. Recognize your shortcomings and work to overcome them instead of blaming other people, life's obstacles, and circumstances.

Maintaining and improving your life in a modern, intricate society requires action; in other words, work - and lots of it. Whether you're collecting trash, waiting on tables, or plotting the trajectory of the next Mars rover, it's all honorable, has to be done, and it takes everyone's efforts.

Adopt a work ethic that recognizes that benefits come from performing honest work that buyers value in the open market. You often become better at your job and qualify yourself for more responsibility and pay through experience from dealing with a variety of situations over time. Whether you stick with a single career or several, make yourself more valuable than what you're being paid for.

When you don't: you become a self-absorbed failure, unable to play a role in larger endeavors. You develop an envious, entitlement, victim mentality. If you receive welfare, you may not realize or admit that resources the government gave to you it took away from others (and government can take away from you). You become dependent on the whims of others. The least productive employees are invariably the first ones fired. Frequent job-hopping may make it tough to gain experience in your field. Be informed before jumping from one job/career to another.

7. Develop and apply **financial literacy**.

Plan and prepare for your personal and family's financial future; prepare and follow a budget to spend below your means and invest for the unexpected – even if you're only saving a small amount each pay period.

Expensive purchases like a vehicle, house, and schooling put you in the market for borrowed money, which you need to shop for as diligently as what you spend it on. Do you qualify for a better rate? Know how to shop for a low-interest loan and realize the impacts of compound interest. Understand consumer debt, credit cards, credit scores, predatory mortgage lenders, and how they impact your financial well-being. It's certainly not as appealing as watching a favorite sports team or a day with the family, but it's crucial for financial well-being.

Within your financial means, maximize employers' contributions to a retirement plan. What are the tax advantages of a Roth IRA? Understand what and how much risk is associated with investments and recognize that larger returns often go hand-in-hand with increased risk. If it's beyond your comfort level, seek a trusted financial advisor or a proven, low-cost financial services company like Vanguard or Fidelity.

Learn how to accumulate wealth through those actions, non-retirement investments, and property ownership. How much will Social Security payments add to your income?

When you don't: You fall victim to expensive scams that rob your earnings and risk a deferred retirement or one of hardship and scarcity. You live in fear of financial calamity from paycheck interruption or unplanned expense, You shift blame to more successful people.

8. Practice a program of **personal well-being**

This covers the high points your mother always told you about: eat a balanced diet, exercise (strength, flexibility, and aerobic), and keep the stress in check. Then avoid risky behaviors like tobacco use, un-prescribed drugs, and immoderate consumption of alcohol.

I've Had Enough!

No unplanned pregnancies or those you cannot afford financially and with the time, care, and love they deserve and require.

<u>When you don't</u>: You become dependent on others for basic activities and support. If you neglect your body, expect others to have to bear the personal and financial consequences for your negligence.

Medical expenses bring you to the verge of financial chaos and you have to severely restrict your activity, diet, and overall quality of life.

While there are surely other behaviors that contribute to success or failure, these eight form a rock-solid foundation that successful people acquire through family, faith, education, work, and life experiences. To fully benefit from these universal behaviors, individuals and the nation have to continually identify and eliminate discrimination based on innate factors of race, gender, age, faith, and sexual orientation.

People who deliberately or otherwise fail to practice fundamentally successful behaviors are essentially saying, "I want all the benefits others enjoy, but I don't want to behave like they do to get them - behaviors that I declare are discriminatory and demeaning or require too much effort. I want to be my unique self, true to my origins, race, gender, faith, sexuality, geographical identity or whatever. And if I don't adopt the behaviors that have achieved success in this society, it must be everyone *else's* fault – they're deplorable racists, sexists, homophobes, misogynists, and xenophobes."

Do they have a point? How can we be confident that practicing successful behaviors is the answer, and those who don't are just victims of old-fashioned discrimination? The answer lies in human history, across the ages in different societies on every continent.

Too often, liberals fail to delve into the *individual's* irresponsibilities and associated failures, but seek ever more-contrived external rationales for personal defeats. Having identified a new college admissions discriminator, like national admission test scores, they clamorously demand that universities dilute or eliminate the standards, allocate ever more money to expand counselling staffs and faculty, or impanel boards of directors with more representation of whichever group is currently complaining the loudest.[157] All wrapped up in the sanctimonious rubric of inclusion, safety, and equality.

Then, we curiously watch them divide students along the exact same racial, ethnic, and orientation lines they'd just howled to erase by operating segregated dormitories, divided student centers, and conducting lavender graduations.

I've had enough.

I've Had Enough!

Chapter 17: What Is Success?

L iving the behaviors in the last chapter promotes improved individual health, security, emotional/psychological balance, and personal satisfaction; in other words, a better quality of life. As more of a society's population adheres to them, the more successful *it* becomes in three fundament ways. Successful societies are able to:

1. **Defend themselves** against external and internal threats. Successful societies accomplish this by committing to a unifying purpose, understanding threats, preparing responses with strengths in depth, and forming coalitions with allied societies.

When they do not: They're significantly oppressed, diminished, or perish. Examples include millions of members of African tribes defeated by other tribes and sold as slaves over centuries. American Indian tribes that couldn't defend themselves against other tribes and the U.S. government. WWII-era Austria, Czechoslovakia, Poland, France, Russia, the Philippines, China, and countless other countries/societies/tribes throughout history paid dearly for their inadequate defenses.

2. **Provide the basic necessities of life** through meaningful, legal employment that enable earners to obtain food, shelter, and health care, as well meet their desire for fulfillment. The government is not responsible for employing people, but for enforcing equal rights to create and operate entities that do. That done, successful societies enforce individuals' equal opportunity to work at those jobs.

When they do not: Populations are mal-nourished, starved, succumb to preventable/treatable diseases, and turn on one another. Crony capitalism and market abuses reduce the quality of life and may lead to revolution and tyranny. Venezuelans have been attempting to reverse their condition for years, but are thwarted because the Maduro regime has strongly embraced success factor #1 above. Socialist/communist Venezuelan, North Korea, and Cuban societies don't adequately feed, clothe, house, and provide for their members' health.

3. **Secure individual liberties.** Free societies open the floodgates for their *entire population* to contribute its thoughts, ideas, and energies, invariably accomplishing more than a limited number of centralized socialist government administrators possibly could.

<u>When societies do not:</u> Powerful people dictate what, when, where, how, and with whom you can live your life, Overall productivity declines and people's quality of life deteriorates. Again, witness Venezuela, Cuba, Russia, North Korea, Syria, Iran, and China, as well as cities that've adopted much more centralized control.

This graph illustrates two groups with their members arrayed according to how many of them practice the behaviors in Chapter 15. Historically, groups whose members practice more of the behaviors will enjoy more success; in this case, Group B will be more successful over time than Group A.

Distribution of Society Members Who Practice Behaviors Associated With Success

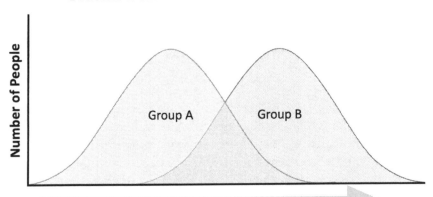

It's important to recognize four key points about the two groups. First, they may be defined by a single characteristic, such as gender or race, or, conversely, no single common factor at all (very diverse). Recognize that even if a group *is* defined by a single characteristic, they also have other individual traits. If the common characteristic is a race or gender, for example, they can also be old or young, highly-educated or not, physically fit or couch potatoes, ambitious or indolent.

Second, the collective members of both groups often practice the same *range* of behaviors. That is, both groups have some members who don't adhere to *any* of the behaviors and some individuals who practice *all* of them (and do so very consistently). The majority of members fall in between these two extremes, and where the bulk of them falls is critically important to the overall group's success.

Third, in a large diverse group or population like ours, the relative positions of groups A and B are not due to skin color, gender, or because they have some innate racial-gender capability to succeed ("white privilege"). Rather, many of them and a number of people of other skin colors and gender learn and adhere to the racial and gender-blind behaviors that are the foundation of more successful individuals in the society. Depending upon the characteristic that defines the groups, you may observe a *correlation* between it and other characteristics. That doesn't mean that the correlated trait is the *cause* of the group's success, however. Absent some outside influence, adherence to key behaviors over time achieves more success.

Fourth. Individuals, and therefore populations, are not forever bound to their current status. Over time, members may adopt more or fewer of the enumerated behaviors, thereby shifting themselves and their population to the right or left. This commonly occurs as members adopt a new/different outlook or attitude; pursue relevant education (formal and informal/study); become more persistent or tenacious; are willing to take on new or greater responsibility; innovation and job creation; mentoring; opportunity; physical and emotional fitness; or when barriers are removed. The lessons of the Scots and the Comanches under Quanah Parker are cases in point.

In our intricate and sophisticated society, those Americans and their descendants who regularly practice more of the behaviors over time will be more successful. Others who are ignorant or uninformed of how to move forward, or who don't invest the considerable effort to do so, will remain on the outside looking in. Many of them will become frustrated and be led by progressives.

Chapter 18: Effecting Change

C hanging society takes considerably more than feelings and empathy, which are both highly subjective and individual. President Trump is disliked, even despised, for bringing change to the federal government - stirring things up (of course, some people just dislike his personality). Established, embedded, and powerful special interests who benefit from crooked government and crony capitalism will strongly rebel against *anyone* who upsets their cozy, lucrative arrangements. The shame is that more elected leaders haven't taken on fights to benefit rank and file Americans.

Liberal educators and administrators have opened a Pandora's box of mob violence in major cities. More expensive diversity and coaching programs are not the answer but a diversion from root problems. America is a very accepting country of its many races, ethnicities and religions and, with the exception of some large cities with decades of liberal leaders, one of the safest.

Activists with no grasp of history or realistic experience about their aspirational socialist/communist societies are bringing too much wasteful attention to the wrong issues, rather than focusing meaningful debate on essential ones.

Education.

Ignorance is a weakness and vulnerability, as the big-bank mortgage scams so amply demonstrated. Education is key; families must support it at home and governments must support parental choices of schools. Slaves who were threatened and horribly mistreated persevered to read and write. Black individuals, their families, and leaders passionately prioritized knowledge during Reconstruction and must unanimously do so again.

There are never sufficient legal measures to prevent the immoral predators of every race to ply their schemes on the vulnerable, often using real or contrived racial differences to advance themselves or a cause. Education is the best defense against them.

The goal of K-12 education is to prepare students with knowledge and ability to begin lives of their own, which may be direct entry into the workforce, attending a trade school or higher education, enlisting in a uniformed service, or a less fiscally remunerative, but self-sustaining, self-satisfying, lawful, pursuit. Regardless of their goals, fundamental financial literacy information is an imperative that's lacking in government schools.

Today, too many students have precious little or no historical or realistic benchmarks to critically judge ideas and situations. Their ideas of what constitutes true fear, safety and overt racism lack such realities as Nazi Germany's murderous tactics of millions of Jews, Gypsies, and Russians. Or American settlers' lethal incursions against Indians.

Well-prepared students can solve problems with critical skills instead of raw, immature, narrowly-based emotions. While many may enter as pampered, inexperienced, entitled, and non-contributing children, they shouldn't graduate as such. Rather than shielding, expose them to challenging ideas, standards, and discipline; suspend, or expel those who are violent or block free speech. Citizens must graduate with an understanding of our government, which enables them to navigate its organization to resolve grievances and assess candidates against Constitutional principles.

That educational system is best achieved when parents, rather than government, determine which schools their children attend. And that requires a break in the teachers' unions' stranglehold on those elected officials who routinely support government control of children. Elect public officials who champion, rather than obstruct, vouchers and charter schools.

Base acceptance to higher education's limited seats on demonstrated academic potential as evidenced by past performance rather than using these institutions for discriminatory social engineering and equal outcomes. To ensure no applicant is discriminated against on the basis of 1964 Civil Rights Act categories of race, color, religion, sex, or national origin, that information should not be available to admissions personnel.

Supreme Court Justice Clarence Thomas in his dissent with the Court's 2003 decision to extend University of Michigan Law School's affirmative action for 25 years: "I believe blacks can achieve in every avenue of American life without the meddling of university administrators. While I agree that in 25 years the practices of the Law School will be illegal, they are, for the reasons I have given, illegal now."

Hire, retain, promote, and dismiss faculty based on their students' demonstrated achievement, instead of longevity, academic certifications, and administrators' desires to balance race, gender, and ethnicity statistics. There are outstanding minorities who qualify and K-12 education and families must develop more of them.

Dissolve academia's diversity structures that promote victimization and impede students' transition to the world at large. Students and faculty who feel aggrieved can present their complaints to the university's original offices to arbitrate such matters: Deans of conduct and admissions, search committees, and security. Eliminate the myriad and very expensive ($210,000 a year) vice chancellors and their layered and overlapping committees.

In higher education, abolish institutionally segregated classes, dormitories, Greeks, and ceremonies so diverse students learn additional life skills and are able to carry on in the face of differences and contrary opinions.

Employment.

Vote for public officials who will repeal legislation protecting crony capitalism. A few open-market state lawmakers, for example, have sided with electric car manufacturer Tesla in allowing factory-direct car sales, while more crony-friendly states like Alabama, Georgia, Virginia, and Texas prohibit the practice.[158] CA legislators bent to pressure requiring ride-sharing companies like UBER to classify volunteer drivers as employees instead of contractors (voters subsequently defeated the measure in a state-wide referendum). All such measures benefit a few at the expense of the overall job market.

Incentivize businesses to locate in/closer to inner cities to provide more jobs consistent with their safety and those residents' skills. Implement dedicated city bus routes from high unemployment urban areas of major job sites (some businesses have already done this on their own.)

Abolish the federal minimum wage, which precludes businesses from hiring low-skilled workers, including those just entering the work force and willing to augment the family's income. These jobs aren't intended as careers or to provide one's sole income.

Abolish preferential hiring and advancement based on race, gender, and ethnicity, while ensuring that hiring and advancement are based on applicants' potential for performance in the desired position. California voters passed proposition 209 with a 10-point margin to accomplish this in public employment, public contracting, and government education 36 years ago. Liberal lawmakers attempted to repeal the measure in 2020 and voters rejected the effort by an even larger margin: 57% - 43%.

Elected Officials

Don't believe what any politician or candidate tells you; examine their actual *record of accomplishments* and how they vote in the legislature. Their central role demands that they support policies, laws, and budgets that advance the actions already presented above.

Many need to re-establish credibility of government institutions, particularly in law enforcement and courts, through continued outreach and publicizing their performance records. A vital part of that is calling out race hucksters and slanted media.

Since many of them won't accomplish these measures of sound government, it's up to their bosses, you the voter, to fire the bad ones and hire more responsive people to replace them.

Other Authority Figures

Pro athletes, actors, artists, and civic leaders have a moral obligation to use their significant celebrity to encourage their followers to understand and follow successful behaviors.

Journalism

As an institution, its members are long overdue to convene a sit-down with their collective conscience to assess journalism's role in our Constitutional republic and how they're failing in that vital responsibility.

Reporters, anchors, and editors are entitled to their personal opinions and to share them as op-eds when they identify them as such. *Professional* journalists distinguish themselves by reporting all the relevant facts instead of just those supporting their personal opinions. Professionals also include opposing voices on issues to provide audiences with different perspectives. Reporters must gather and report actual facts instead of publicizing inflammatory emotional outbursts; be the adult in the room.

Consider this mendacious August 8, 2019 Associated Press headline story of the incident in Ferguson, MO,

> FERGUSON, Mo. (AP) — On Aug. 9, 2014, Michael Brown and a friend were walking in the middle of Canfield Drive, a two-lane street in the St. Louis suburb of Ferguson, Missouri when a police officer drove by and told them to use the sidewalk.
>
> "After words were exchanged, the white officer confronted the 18-year-old Brown, who was black. The situation escalated, with the officer and Brown scuffling. The officer shot and killed Brown, who was unarmed.[159]

Note how it begins with "a police officer drove by and told them to use the sidewalk", making it sound like the cop was on the prowl, spotted his prey, and started demanding obedience. The truth was nothing of the sort. A police officer didn't just "drive by and tell two black youths to use the sidewalk." As explained in Chapter 11, Michael had stolen merchandise from a convenience store and assaulted the cashier mere minutes before, prompting the cashier's daughter to report the crimes. The reporter wrongly and negligently omits those very pertinent contextual facts.

You'll recall that police quickly broadcast the crime and description of the suspect; a nearby officer immediately spotted Brown and his friend with the stolen merchandise in hand. 6'4" 295 lb. Brown was repeatedly non-compliant with the officer's lawful requests, leaned into the police vehicle, vigorously assaulted the sitting officer, and fought to take his service pistol in the process. That felonious act is much more serious than the "scuffle" reported by the AP. Outside of the vehicle, Brown charged the officer several more times after failing to heed the officer's orders. The AP reporter significantly downplayed Brown's role by writing "The situation escalated".

The news media also jumped on reports that Brown, at a distance from the officer, held his hands up and plead, "Don't shoot." Under oath, witnesses changed their story and said no such thing happened; Brown deliberately assaulted the officer.

This is another clear case of completely deceitful, biased, inaccurate reporting by a supposedly professional news source. It completely failed to live up to The Journalists' Creed on a bronze plaque hanging in the National Press Club in Washington, D.C. that includes this tenet,

> "I believe that the public journal is a public trust; that all connected with it are, to the full measure of their responsibility, trustees for the public; that acceptance of a lesser service than the public service is betrayal of this trust."

Too many reporters and their editors have betrayed that very core trust. Journalists: respect and adhere to your creed.

Vagrancy

"Homeless" describes a *consequence* of conditions that affect some 567,000 Americans, rather than the essence of the people themselves or the basis of their status. The folksy term is tailored to tug at the emotional heartstrings, but fails to highlight the multiple causes of inadequate food, clothing, and more substantial and secure shelter than a sleeping bag, park bench, cardboard box, or tent. The destitute may, however, also be defined by negative or aimless cultures and attitudes they've actively or unconsciously adopted, mental or physical maladies, or severe setbacks and traumas.

Everyone has to be somewhere, either on property owned privately, by a tribe, or governments. If there're unable to rent or buy their own place and they aren't in a tribe, they end up on the only remaining land left: government property - parks, underpasses, sidewalks, and the like.

Without toilets, facilities to clean themselves and clothing, and inadequate garbage service, they create a health problem for themselves and those who may come in contact with them and their encampments. Their slovenly lifestyle disrupts nearby small businesses earning money for their own families. Such dispersed living also makes it more difficult for government, faith, and service organizations to effectively assist and protect them from further abuse and predators.

Addressing their fundamental issues like mental disorders, lack of education, alcoholism, drug addiction, illness, or insolvency, is a complex and resource-intensive effort that may never be completely accomplished. Here, however, is a step to accommodate that portion of the population pending their transition to a better life. The idea is to create safer low-cost, low maintenance neighborhoods where these populations can live at no cost to them.

Solicit corporate sponsors, such as Google and Facebook, to augment government funding for initial construction and sustained maintenance. Neighborhoods would consist of paved lanes with drainage for pressure-washing to facilitate cleaning and disinfecting. Between the lanes are slightly raised cement personal paddocks that are slightly peaked for drainage. Paddocks include recessed eyebolts for residents to secure their tents and possessions.

Overhead vandal-proof sun/rain covers provide a degree of protection from rains and intense sun. Strategically-placed facilities within the neighborhood include:
- Fresh water spigots
- Banks of concrete/steel toilets and urinals
- Shower stalls
- Trash receptacles
- Hearty trees on the perimeter and interior
- Nearby access to transportation

Additionally, perimeter office-type spaces would be included for:
- Counsellors for residents with physical & mental health, drug, and alcohol issues
- Health clinics
- Receiving, storing, and distributing food donations from residents, grocers, bakeries, and restaurants
- Receiving financial donations from the public, faith, charitable, and service organizations, as well as corporate sponsors
- Clothing receipt, sorting, and disbursement

I've Had Enough!

- Education, job training and placement workers
- VA offices

Concurrent with developing the neighborhood is the parallel action to enact local ordinances prohibiting elimination in public, loitering, panhandling, and establishing personal accommodations outside the neighborhoods (like in parks). Recurrent violators would be subject to jail or commitment to appropriate mental health institutions as determined by competent authority.

The municipality should provide a two-week transition period to vacate camps currently outside the designated neighborhoods, with the option to locate in a public neighborhood. Government and private entities could assist moving people to the neighborhoods, and restore public sanitation/health conditions in vacated areas. Following the transition period, government would involuntarily re-locate violators and their possessions to the public neighborhoods.

It would also be useful to residents and administrators alike to develop and publicize incentives for residents who make progress at becoming self-sufficient within or outside the neighborhood. What are the incentives? Better conditions. These may be as basic as selecting a site closer to bathrooms (or farther away if they prefer).

The neighborhoods themselves wouldn't rehabilitate residents, but would facilitate centralized availability of resources to help with rehabilitation, provide a cleaner, healthier, and safer environment at an affordable price to the government and the public.

Wokeness

Woke liberals decide issues emotionally, how they "feel", to a much greater extent than employing a critical evaluation of evidence and truths. Progressives jump on correlations rather than causes, they regularly overlook the realities and dimensions of human nature and appear to be generally illiterate in history. Their extensive culture of victimology ignores any of the perceived victims' personal failings, inadequate academic preparation, envy, and frustrations with their life that they can't control or that require real effort.

The trending causes now are social and economic justice, which often translates into "Give me what someone else has earned". Liberal wokes dissect every imaginable human action, contrive a linkage to race or lifestyle, then identify related "microaggressions", unconscious bias, and inject a need for "trigger warnings" to protect delicate souls from dealing with reality. Connecting any of their findings with the running narrative of police-brutality further increases peer sympathy, agreement, and admiration.

Next up on a woke's agenda are speaking tours, interviews by CNN's Don Lemon, hosting expensive seminars and workshops to minutely examine some arcane factor that makes little, if any, real difference. All the while, inner cities burn, Black-on-Black crime kills thousands annually, too many minorities fail to acquire academic proficiency for legitimate college admissions, graduation, and landing desired jobs.

The woke squads are completely out of touch with foundational American values of personal freedom, self-reliance, free-enterprise, and smaller, less intrusive government. Actually, they despise these values and Americans who support them.

Wokes have too much time on their hands without having to face *real* adversity (go to Venezuela for a month). Many were indoctrinated by years of professors with intellectual cravings and their own need for recognition through discovery of a bias and a way to measure and connect it to a current trendy narrative. Typically, their social theories lack empirical evidence and they pay no price for failure.

Achieving wisdom includes the consideration of opposing ideas and debating their merits and faults against your own, which they rarely do.

Black Families and Culture

Dignity, honor, and success, like the U.S. Marines' lapel insignia, are earned, never given. In our context, "earning" is excelling (or at least not lagging) in education and personal and professional pursuits. Doing so earns self-respect and, over time and associations with others, earns their respect as well. That doesn't suggest we forget history, but consider the past in a balanced perspective that allows a productive focus on the present.

Across every race and ethnicity, family is the basic unit of a developed society. Its reconstitution is essential where education, income, and crime evidence show it has significantly weakened. Strong, tightly-knit black families were a prevalent foundation for achievement and success when discrimination was much worse than it is now. The poverty rate among Blacks fell from 87% in 1940 to 47% by 1960. Over the next 20 years it dropped another 18% - a continuation of the preceding trend rather than liberal policies espoused by liberal spokespeople.[160] Many families like that still thrive, but information presented in Chapter 9 shows us the foundation is absent in too many others. The prevalence of a "ghetto culture" of crime, hatred and derision, disdain for education, and contempt for assimilating into productive society has had devastating effects. Rebuilding requires changed attitudes as well as help.

Families play a major role in developing children's attitudes about faith, morality, other people, government, families, and work. Deep-seated opinions about slavery, other races, privilege, and debts owed them are not exempt. What attitudes about hate or love, acceptance or hostility, fear or confidence are parents teaching their children? Will it perpetuate division or develop leaders to overcome it? To paraphrase former Israeli Prime Minister Golda Meir, "Peace will come when we love our children more than we hate others."

Here're two perspectives, the first is from professional basketball superstar LeBron James, who grew up not knowing his father:

"Black men, Black women, Black kids, we are terrified. Because you don't know, you have no idea. You have no idea how that cop that day left the house. You don't know if he woke up on the good side of the bed, you don't know if he woke up on the wrong side of the bed."

Black father Patrick D. Hampton responded to LeBron:

R.J. Ross

Dear LeBron James,

You don't speak for me and my boys.
I'm a father of four brown boys. It is my responsibility as a father to protect and serve them. There is no need for police in my home because as the father, I'm the authority in my home.

Police are needed where fathers and law and order are absent. When there is no father to protect and serve children, police have to move into that community to protect and serve.

Where there is no father or authority in the home or neighborhood, young men rebel. This is why police are having a hard time gaining compliance with fatherless boys on the side of the road. They refuse to sit down, be quiet, and comply. Why? Because the police are the first men to tell them NO and assert their authority. These boys have spent years under no one's authority. This is the main problem.

So please don't speak for me and my boys. Me and my boys are not terrified of the police because we respect the police and accept their authority. That's because they first had to respect me as their father and accept my authority. Actually, one of them wants to be a police officer. You Lebron are trying to destroy that dream by painting police officers in a negative light when most are good guys.

We are terrified of the black men that kill each other in their black neighborhoods every day. We are afraid of the black men that threaten us and call us cūns and uncle toms for desiring to live a peaceful and successful life. We are aware of the fact that 93% of all black homicides are by black men (Bureau of Justice Statistics).

If you really want to help fatherless boys like yourself, stop using fear tactics and guilt trips. Help promote legislation like "EQUAL SHARED PARENTING" that helps divorced dads and single dads have more time with their children without paying more child support.

I've Had Enough!

How much attention to a very few high-profile interracial incidents is enough? Does it become a sine-qua-non for attention and action to the detriment of a more balanced view and efforts? Is it like the country description about a pot of crap, "the more you stir it, the more it stinks"? When panel host asked Morgan Freeman what to do about racism, the Academy Award winner simply replied "Stop taking about it. I'm going to stop calling you a white man and I'm going to ask you to stop calling me a black man. I know you as Mike Wallace. You know me as Morgan Freeman."

Government had a very mixed record of ensuring equality for the powerless, from outright discrimination at one extreme to ratification of Constitutional amendments at the other. But government is composed of its officials, and too many typify empowered humans who abuse their position to the detriment of those they're sworn to serve. Consequently, Americans, especially minorities, are suspect that government will adequately and consistently guard their rights. And nearly all Americans lack a basic understanding of the institution's purpose, structure, and how to affect change within it; how many know the President's seven enumerated Constitutional authorities?

What should government do? Federal and appropriate state governments must constantly and vigorously uphold anti-discrimination amendments and laws.

Governments could also recognize past major lapses to meet our ideals through official statements that recognize the defect and commit to prohibiting any such recurrence. In doing so, they should also recount the numerous and significant steps taken to more closely achieve that end. After all, ancestors in good standing from our earliest times opposed discrimination and injustices and hundreds of thousands died in the efforts.

Simply *dictating* attitude changes doesn't work; humans are too primal to disregard instincts and quickly overcome prejudices they've grown up with and the daily news frequently validates. The better way forward, as difficult and lengthy as it may be, is to change those who *generate* the fears and prejudices, and expose those who *hold* prejudices to the many better examples of people they wrongly label.

Morgan Freeman's movie character Red Redding in *The Shawshank Redemption* had great advice for fellow convict friend Andy Dufresne, "Get on with living, or get on with dying". In that spirit, it's incumbent on all Americans to

"Get on with ignorance, or get on with learning."
"Get on with failure, or get on with success."
"Get on with your past, or get on with your future."

It's not Americans' essential nature to woefully wring our hands in despair, whine, and lament our status. For so many years through so many tumultuous domestic and world events we've all faced the challenges, innovated, overcome, and progressed – leading the world in the process and shall continue doing so.

Works Consulted

Books

Frederick Bastiat, The Law (Kindle edition)

Kathleen Brush, Racism and anti-Racism in the world: before and after 1945 (Bowker, August 2020)

Jack Cashill, Zimmerman Suit Spells Trouble for Black Lives Matter (The American Spectator, August 2020). Retrieved from https://spectator.org/zimmerman-suit-trayvon-martin-black-lives-matter/

W.E.B. Du Bois, The Souls of Black Folk (Millennium Publications, 2014)

W.E.B. Du Bois, The Health and Physique of the Negro American (Atlanta University Press,1906), Atlanta, GA

Heather Mac Donald, The Diversity Delusion (New York, St. Martin's Press, 2018)

S.C. Gwynne, Empire of the Summer Moon (Scribner, 2011)

Dr. Everett Piper, Not A Day Care, The Devastating Consequences of Abandoning Truth (Salem Books, 2017)

Star Parker, Uncle Sam's Plantation (Thomas Nelson, 2010)

Rachel Parker Plummer, 21 Months A Captive: Rachel Plummer Parker and the Fort Parker Massacre (Annotated) (Independently published 2016)

Rachel Plummer, 21 Months A Captive: Rachel Plummer and the Fort Parker Massacre (Big Byte Books, 2016). Kindle edition

Jason Riley, Please Stop Helping Us (Encounter Books, Kindle edition, 2016)

I've Had Enough!

Jason Riley, False Black Power? (Templeton Press, Kindle edition, 2017)

Richard Rothstein, The Color of Law, a Forgotten History of How Our Government Segregated America (Liveright, 2017, Kindle edition)

William L. Shirer, The Rise and Fall of the Third Reich (Rosetta Books, Kindle edition, October 2011)

Thomas Sowell, Discrimination and Disparities (Basic Books, Kindle edition, revised March 2019)

Thomas Sowell, Black Rednecks and White Liberals (Encounter Books, 2009)

Parker, Star. Uncle Sam's Plantation (Thomas Nelson, August 2010) Kindle Edition.

Shelby Steele, White Guilt (Harper Perennial, reprint 2007 Kindle edition)

David Whitley, George Zimmerman's 'appalling' lawsuit poses legitimate questions| Commentary (Orlando Sentinel, Dec 2019) Retrieved from https://www.orlandosentinel.com/opinion/columnists/os-op-george-zimmerman-lawsuit-david-whitley-20191212-zzpertrd6jailentbko7x6cmum-story.html

Articles, Reports, and Documents

John Cloud, "What Dos SAT Stand For?" (Time Magazine, June 2001). Retrieved from http://content.time.com/time/magazine/article/0,9171,136829,00.html

Ta-Nahesi Coates, "The Case For Reparations" (The Atlantic, June 2014)

Shawn Fremstad; Glynn; Sara Jane; Angelo Williams, Angelo, "The Case Against Marriage Fundamentalism" (Family Story, 2019)

R.J. Ross

Henry Louis Gates Jr., "Slavery by the Numbers" (The Root, 2014). Retrieved from https://www.theroot.com/slavery-by-the-numbers-1790874492

Wesley Lowery, "Study finds police fatally shoot unarmed black men at disproportionate rates" (The Washington Post, April 7, 2016). Retrieved from https://www.washingtonpost.com/national/study-finds-police-fatally-shoot-unarmed-black-men-at-disproportionate-rates/2016/04/06/e494563e-fa74-11e5-80e4-c381214de1a3_story.html?utm_term=.d02307b74429

Heather Mac Donald, "Hey, Ninnies-Grow Up!" (City Journal, Manhattan Institute of Policy Research), March, 2016.

Adaobi Tricia Nwaubani, "When the Slave Traders Were African" (The Wall Street Journal, 2019). Retrieved from https://www.wsj.com/articles/when-the-slave-traders-were-african-11568991595

Rashawn Ray, Andre M. Perry, "Why we need reparations for Black Americans" (Brookings Institute, April 2020). Retrieved from https://www.brookings.edu/policy2020/bigideas/why-we-need-reparations-for-black-americans/

Jenna Ross, "The Racial Wealth Gap in America: Asset Types Held by Race" (Visual Capitalist, 2020). Retrieved from https://www.visualcapitalist.com/racial-wealth-gap/

Evan Sayet, The Woke Supremacy, An Anti-Socialst Manifesto (independently published, Aug, 2020)

Jacob M. Schlesinger, "Two Economists Fuel Democratic Debate Over How Far Left To Go" (The Wall Street Journal, July 14, 2019)

Michael Taylor, Britain's role in slavery was not to end it, but to thwart abolition at every turn (The Guardian, June, 2020)

I've Had Enough!

Dennis Tueller, "How Close is Too Close?" (The Police Policy Studies Council). Retrieved from http://www.theppsc.org/Staff_Views/Tueller/How.Close.htm

U.S. DOJ, "Department of Justice Report Regarding the Criminal Investigation Into the Shooting Death of Michael Brown By Ferguson, Missouri Police Officer Darren Wilson" (U.S. Government Printing Office, Washington, D.C., 2015)

U.S. DOJ, "Investigation of the Ferguson Police Department," (U.S. Government Printing Office, Washington, D.C., March 4, 2015)

Sharmila Choudhury, "Racial and Ethnic Difference in Wealth and Asset Choices" (U.S. Social Security Administration, 2001/2002). Retrieved from https://www.ssa.gov/policy/docs/ssb/v64n4/v64n4p1.html

Gillian B. White, "The Data Are Damning: How Race Influences School Funding" (The Atlantic, September 30, 2015). Retrieved from https://www.theatlantic.com/business/archive/2015/09/public-school-funding-and-the-role-of-race/408085/

Principle Web Sites

Brownfield, A. (2015, July 14) *Sin of Contemporaneity: Cleansing History By Applying Today's Standards To Our Ancestors*. Retrieved from https://humanevents.com/2015/07/14/sin-of-contemporaneity-cleansing-history-by-applying-todays-standards-to-our-ancestors/

Campaign Zero, We can end police violence in America. https://www.joincampaignzero.org/#vision
And its Campaign8 project, https://8cantwait.org

The Centers for Disease Control, *Fatal Injury Reports, National, Regional, and State, 1981 - 2018*. Retrieved from https://webappa.cdc.gov/sasweb/ncipc/mortrate.html https://wisqars.cdc.gov:8443/nvdrs/nvdrsDisplay.jsp https://guncite.com/CDCStats/us9794_homili.htm

Chicago Police Department (2020, October) *Crime Statistics*. Retrieved from https://home.chicagopolice.org/statistics-data/crime-statistics/

Chicago Police Department *JC133190 Redacted and Scanned 1 of 2* (2019, January). Retrieved from tps://www.scribd.com/document/403362913/JC133190-Redacted-and-Scanned-1-of-2

The College Boards *SAT Suite of Assessments Annual Report* (2019). Retrieved from https://reports.collegeboard.org/pdf/2019-total-group-sat-suite-assessments-annual-report.pdf

Comprehensive index of evidence in Jussie Smollett case: https://chicagopolicepublic.blob.core.usgovcloudapi.net/smollett/index.html

Eugene R. Dattel, *Cotton in a Global Economy (1800-1860* (2006, October). Retrieved from http://mshistorynow.mdah.state.ms.us/articles/161/cotton-in-a-global-economy-mississippi-1800-1860

The Economics of Cotton. Retrieved from https://courses.lumenlearning.com/ushistory1os2xmaster/chapter/the-economics-of-cotton/

Cotton Production in the United States. Retrieved from https://en.wikipedia.org/wiki/Cotton_production_in_the_United_States

I've Had Enough!

William Darity Jr. and A. Kirsten Mullen, *How Reparations for American descendants of slavery could narrow the racial wealth divide* (2019). Retrieved from https://www.nbcnews.com/think/opinion/how-reparations-american-descendants-slavery-could-narrow-racial-wealth-divide-ncna1019691

David Eltis, David Richardson, and editors, *The Trans-Atlantic Slave Trade Database.* Retrieved from https://www.slavevoyages.org

Department of the Treasury, Internal Revenue Service. Retrieved from https://www.irs.gov/statistics/soi-tax-stats-individual-statistical-tables-by-tax-rate-and-income-percentile

Federal Bureau of Investigation, *Uniform Crime Reporting Program.* Retrieved from https://ucr.fbi.gov/crime-in-the-u.s/2018/crime-in-the-u.s.-2018

Slavery In History. Retrieved from https://www.freetheslaves.net/about-slavery/slavery-in-history/

Devon Link (2020, June 16) *Fact check: Yes, Kente cloths were historically worn by empire involved in West African slave trade.* Retrieved from https://www.usatoday.com/story/news/factcheck/2020/06/16/fact-check-kente-cloths-have-ties-west-african-slave-trade/5345941002/

Vanessa Northington Gamble and Deborah Stone (2006) *Disparities, Research, and Action: The Historical Context.* Retrieved from https://academic.udayton.edu/health/11Disparities/Disparities07.htm

State of Homelessness: 2020 Edition. (2020 (National Alliance To End Homelessness). Retrieved from https://endhomelessness.org/homelessness-in-america/homelessness-statistics/state-of-homelessness-2020/

Life of Privilege Explained in a $100 Race (Youngsterdam Dynamo, July 2019). Retrieved from https://www.youtube.com/watch?v=kyl4EJhq47A

Beatrice Peterson and Matthew Vann (2019) *Ta-Nehisi Coates and Danny Glover join renewed debate over reparations on Capitol Hill.* Retrieved from https://abcnews.go.com/Politics/debate-reparations-slavery-renewed-capitol-hill/story?id=63793226

Prices and Wages by Decade: 1800-1809. Retrieved from https://libraryguides.missouri.edu/pricesandwages/1800-1809

Roy Beck, *World Poverty, Immigration, and Gumballs* (2017, July 18). Retrieved from https://www.youtube.com/watch?v=FlVMW7g5QBI

Don Popp, Honestly... Semi-random thoughts toward "an honest discussion on race (RenewAmerica, August 5, 2013). Retrieved from http://www.renewamerica.com/columns/popp/130805

Peace Preparatory Academy. Retrieved from https://peaceprep.com

Jonathan Raymond, *What is redlining, and how did it happen in Atlanta?* (2020, February 20). Retrieved from https://www.11alive.com/article/news/community/redlining-at-lan what-it-is-and-impact/85-ad009153-7f8c-4d74-82b7-1d096e9e9b00

Natalie Hope McDonald *All Your Questions About Jussie Smollett's New Indictment Answered* (2020, February 20). Retrieved from https://www.vulture.com/2020/02/jussie-smollet-attack-hoax-arrest-dropped-charges-explained.html

Michael Taylor, *Britain's role in slavery was not to end it, but to thwart abolition at every turn* (2020, June 20). Retrieved from https://www.theguardian.com/commentis-free/2020/jun/20/gladstone-wellington-peel-britain-pro-slavery-british-history-abolition

I've Had Enough!

Troost, William (2008, June 5) The Freedmen's Bureau. Retrieved from http://eh.net/encyclopedia/the-freedmens-bureau/

Our Black Ancestry. Retrieved from https://ourblackancestry.com/about.php

Types of Law Enforcement Agencies, Retrieved from https://www.discoverpolicing.org/explore-the-field/types-of-law-enforcement-agencies/

United Nations General Assembly, *The Universal Declaration of Human Rights* (1948, December). Retrieved from https://www.un.org/en/universal-declaration-human-rights/index.html

The U.S. Census Bureau, (2020). Retrieved from https://www.census.gov

Julie Tate, Jennifer Jenkins, Steven Rich (2020) Fatal Force. Retrieved from https://www.washingtonpost.com/graphics/investigations/police-shootings-database/

https://www.reuters.com/article/us-usa-yale-discrimination-idUSKCN2592YT

Evan Gerstmann, *Why The Asian American Students Lost Their Case Against Harvard (But Should Have Won.* (2019, October) Retrieved from https://www.forbes.com/sites/evangerstmann/2019/10/01/why-the-asian-american-students-lost-their-case-against-harvard-but-should-have-won/#3a16c5a963c1

Leslie M. Harris, *The New York City Draft Riots of 1863* (2003) Retrieved from https://press.uchicago.edu/Misc/Chicago/317749.html&title=The+New+York+City+Draft+Riots+of+1863&desc=

About the Author

Bob Ross accumulated a variety of experiences growing up in the Caribbean, California, and Florida, where he attended the University of Florida. As a land grant college, ROTC was mandatory for physically fit males; it was, after all, the '60s and the Viet Nam War was raging half a world away. A modest cadet stipend and part-time job helped pay room and board.

On the same day he graduated with a BS in Business Administration, the Army commissioned him a 2nd Lieutenant of Armor. Following training at Fort Knox, KY and Fort Benning, GA, the Army assigned him to Fort Lee, VA.

Subsequent assignments took the Rosses to Army posts throughout the continental United States, Hawaii, the Republic of Panama, Bolivia, Honduras, South Korea, Thailand, Japan, Egypt, Kuwait, and a tour on the Joint Staff at the Pentagon during the First Gulf War. Bob completed a master's degree in Inventory Management and a Senior Officials in National Security fellowship at Harvard's JFK School of Government.

He retired as a colonel, then started and ran his own consulting business for seven years before pursuing digital photography and earning his FAA drone pilot certification.

In GA, Ross also worked with another equally concerned citizen and several allies to replace all five county commissioners, two school board members, a mayor, a city councilman, and the county sheriff. At the state level, the Atlanta Journal Constitution newspaper described him as "A pillar of the [anti-sales tax increase] campaign."

Bob met and married Joye, the daughter of a WWII combat veteran and engaging low-country South Carolina farmer. Their son and daughter achieved Boy Scout Eagle rank and Girl Scout Gold Award status respectively. Bob and his wife regularly enjoy spending time with their five grandchildren.

I've Had Enough!

End Notes

[1] Corina Pons, <u>Update 1-Venezuela 2016 inflation hits 800 pct, GDP contracts nearly 19 pct</u> (Reuters, Jan 20 2017).
https://www.reuters.com/article/venezuela-economy-idUSL1N1FA1JL
World Bank, 2015 poverty value is the most recent. Retrieved from https://data.worldbank.org/indicator/SI.POV.NAHC?locations=VE
Murder rate in Venezuela, 56/100,000 vs. 5.6 in U.S.
https://www.macrotrends.net/countries/VEN/venezuela/murder-homicide-rate

[2] <u>U.S. Poverty Rate, 1974-2021</u> (Macrotrends). https://www.macrotrends.net/countries/USA/united-states/poverty-rate

[3] Supreme Court Justice Oliver Wendell Holmes' address to the Suffolk Bar Association.

[4] <u>U.S. Public Becoming Less Religious</u>, (Pew Research Center, November 3, 2015.

[5] John Lyde Wilson, <u>The Code of Honor; or Rules for the Government of Principals and Seconds in Dueling</u> (James Phinney, Charleston, South Carolina, 1858) page 42. Retrieved from https://archive.org/details/codeofhonoror-rul00wils/page/42/mode/2up

[6] Seattle Police Chief Carmen Best's July 23, 2020 letter to Seattle City Council members, https://spdblotter.seattle.gov/2020/07/23/letter-to-city-council-regarding-council-ordinance-119805-crowd-control-tools-%EF%BB%BF/

[7] Eric Johnson, <u>Seattle City Council mulls law that could result in dismissal of many misdemeanor crimes</u> (KOMO News, October 26, 2020). Retrieved from https://komonews.com/news/local/seattle-city-council-mulls-plan-that-could-result-in-dismissal-of-many-misdemeanor-crimes

[8] Crime Dashboard, 2020, Seattle Police Department. Retrieved Jan 2, 2021 from http://www.seattle.gov/police/information-and-data/crime-dashboard

[9] David Sirota, What's the Difference Between a Liberal and a Progressive? (HUFFPOST, May 5, 2011)

[10] Notable liberals who openly support the violent organization Antifa's actions include Minneapolis City Councilman Jeremiah Ellison (son of the state's Attorney General) and Seattle City Councilwoman Tammy Morales. Portland, OR Mayor Ted Wheeler publicly supported over a 100 days of city protests, even after repeated acts of violence.

[11] Alan Gallay, Indian Slavery in the Americas (The Gilder Lehrman Institute of American History). Retrieved from https://ap.gilderlehrman.org/essay/indian-slavery-americas

[12] Mychal Massie, What if Africans had stayed in Africa? (The Daily Rant, July 2020). Retrieved from https://mychal-massie.com/what-if-africans-had-stayed-in-africa/

[13] World's Billionaire List (Forbes magazine). Retrieved from https://www.forbes.com/billionaires/
And
The World Factbook, (Central Intelligence Agency). Retrieved from https://www.cia.gov/library/publications/resources/the-world-factbook/fields/221.html

[14] U.S. Bureau of Labor Statistics, Business Employment Dynamics, Entrepreneurship and the U.S. Economy, Establishment survival, chart 3. https://www.bls.gov/bdm/entrepreneurship/entrepreneurship.htm

[15] Census Bureau Reports at Least 350 Languages Spoken in U.S. Homes (U.S. Census Bureau, Nov 3, 2013). Retrieved from https://www.census.gov/newsroom/press-releases/2015/cb15-185.html
Membership of U.S. religious & spiritual groups (Religious

Tolerance, 2003). Retrieved from http://www.religioustoler-ance.org/us_rel1.htm)

[16] Nine representatives from as many countries drafted the Declaration; the U.S. drafter was Eleanor Roosevelt – wife of President Franklin Delano Roosevelt.

[17] There is a single mention of "democratic participation" in para 3.2 of United Nations Conference on Environment & Development (United Nations, NY, NY, 1992), Agenda 21

[18] United Nations Conference on Environment & Development (United Nations, NY, NY, 1992), Agenda 21 , Ch 33, para 33.18

[19] Larry Bell, "Blood and Gore: Making A Killing On Anti-Carbon Investment Hype" (Forbes, Nov 2013) https://www.forbes.com/sites/larrybell/2013/11/03/blood-and-gore-making-a-killing-on-anti-carbon-investment-hype/#76a8729a32dc

Corey Barnes, The Money and Connections Behind Al Gore's Carbon Crusade (Human Events, October 3, 2007). Retrieved from https://humanevents.com/2007/10/03/the-money-and-connections-behind-al-gores-carbon-crusade/

[20] 116th Congress (2019-2020), House Resolution 109 and Senate Resolution 59

[21] State of the Global Climate 2020, Provisional Report (United Nations' World Meteorological Organization, undated). Retrieved from https://library.wmo.int/doc_num.php?explnum_id=10444

[22] Rebecca Lindsey, LuAnn Dahlman, Climate Change: Global Temperature (national Oceanic and Atmospheric Administration, August 14, 2020). Retrieved from https://www.climate.gov/news-features/understanding-climate/climate-change-global-temperature

[23] Debate sponsored by the The Heartland Institute; https://youtu.be/b8JZo6PzpCU

[24] https://www.prageru.com/video/climate-change-what-do-scientists-say/

[25] Ed Adamczyk, Navy chief calls China the greatest threat, proposes more warships ((UPI, Oct 14, 2020). Retrieved from https://www.upi.com/Defense-News/2020/10/14/Navy-chief-calls-China-the-greatest-threat-proposes-more-warships/5961602700705/

[26] Jocelyn Grzeszczak, 81% of Black Americans Don't Want Less Police Presence Despite Protests – Some Want More Cops (Newsweek, Aug 6, 2020). Retrieved from https://www.newsweek.com/81-black-americans-dont-want-less-police-presence-despite-protestssome-want-more-cops-poll-1523093

[27] Stephen T. Parente, Roger Feldman, Jean Abraham, Yi Xu, Consumer Response to a National Marketplace for Individual Insurance, (U.S. Department of Health and Human Services, 2008), page 8, https://aspe.hhs.gov/system/files/pdf/75826/report.pdf

[28] Yaron Steinbuch, Iowa State professor forced to change syllabus after banning criticism of BLM (New York Post, August 19, 2020)

[29] President Obama pontificated to an adoring crowd in Roanoke, VA in 2012.

[30] Jason Daley, First Humans Entered the Americas Along the Coast, Nor Through the Ice, (Smithsonian Magazine, 2016), https://www.smithsonianmag.com/smart-news/humans-colonized-americas-along-coast-not-through-ice-180960103/

[31] Human Origins 101, (National Geographic, 2018), https://www.youtube.com/watch?v=ehV-MmuvVMU

[32] Ellis Island Medals of Honor Archive. Retrieved from http://medalists.eihonors.org/index.html

[33] https://www.lifenews.com/2020/08/17/study-liberal-media-has-150-times-more-negative-coverage-of-president-trump-than-joe-biden/

[34] Barbara Ortutay, David Klepper, Twitter and Facebook suspend Trump's accounts after violence at US Capitol (Chicago Tribune, Jan 7, 2021). Retrieved from https://www.chicagotribune.com/nation-world/ct-nw-trump-twitter-suspended-20210107-labnvknuv5alxduavcb5mgmhum-story.html

[35] J. Clara Chan, Twitter Permanently Suspends Trump's Account (The Wrap, Jan 8, 2021). Retrieved from https://www.thewrap.com/twitter-permanently-suspends-trumps-account/

[36] Li Cohen, Twitter and Facebook lock Trump's accounts, take down video of his message to supporters (CBS News, Jan 7, 2021). Retrieved from https://www.cbsnews.com/news/trump-twitter-facebook-accounts-locked/

[37] Campaign contributions by The National Education Association, about $20m, and the American Federation of Teachers, about $12m, hit an all-time high in 2016, with virtually all of it going to Democrats and liberal groups. https://www.opensecrets.org/industries/indus.php?ind=L1300

[38] Susan Edelman, Mayor DeBlasio is firing fewer teachers accused of misconduct (New York Post, Nov 2, 2019). Retrieevd from https://nypost.com/2019/11/02/mayor-de-blasio-is-firing-fewer-teachers-accused-of-misconduct/

[39] https://wp.rutgers.edu/gwp/gwp-home

[40] Justice Department Files Statement of Interest in California Campus Speech Case (U.S. Department of Justice, October 24, 2017). Retrieved from https://www.justice.gov/opa/pr/justice-department-files-statement-interest-california-campus-speech-case

And
Perry Chiaramonte, <u>LA college district abolishes free speech zones as part of lawsuit settlement</u> (FoxNews.com, December 14, 2018). Retrieved from https://www.foxnews.com/us/la-college-district-abolishes-free-speech-zones-as-part-of-lawsuit-settlement

[41] Bestselling New York Times conservative writer and noted speaker Heather Mac Donald documents numerous such incidents in her book <u>The Diversity Delusion</u> (St. Martin's Press, 2018)

[42] U.S. Department of Education, Campus Safety and Security, https://ope.ed.gov/campussafety/#/compare/search

[43] Dude, <u>How Many Genders Are There In 2020?</u> https://dudeasks.com/how-many-genders-are-there-in-2020/

[44] The Official Website of the City of New York/Office of the Mayor/News/December 21, 2015: https://www1.nyc.gov/office-of-the-mayor/news/961-15/nyc-commission-human-rights-strong-protections-city-s-transgender-gender

[45] Barbara Hollingsworth, <u>University of Michigan Student's Designated Pronoun is 'His Majesty'</u> (CNS News, 2016), https://www.cnsnews.com/blog/barbara-hollingsworth/university-michigan-students-designated-pronoun-his-majesty

[46] Ralph Luker, <u>On Marin Luther King's Plagiarism...</u> (Columbian College of Arts & Sciences, 2004). Retrieved from https://historynewsnetwork.org/blog/9172

[47] Eric Pianin, <u>A Senator's Shame</u> (Washington Post, 2005), Robert C. Byrd, in a letter to Sen. Theodore Bilbo (D-MS), 1944; https://web.archive.org/web/20071117055016/http://www.washingtonpost.com/wp-dyn/content/article/2005/06/18/AR2005061801105_pf.html

[48] Martin Schram, Sen. Byrd: Conscience of the Senate? (Kitsap Sun, June 2005). Retrieved from https://products.kitsap-sun.com/archive/2005/06-24/54211_sen__byrd__conscience_of_the_sen.html

[49] Scottie Andrew, Harmeet Kaur, Everyday words and phrases that have racist connotations (CNN, 2020) https://www.cnn.com/2020/07/06/us/racism-words-phrases-slavery-trnd/index.html

[50] Appendix A, Inclusive Language (University of Michigan, 2020). Retrieved from https://injurycenter.umich.edu/opioid-overdose/michigan-safer-opioid-prescribing-toolkit/background-on-opioid-use-pain-and-pain-management/reducing-stigma/words-matter/
And
https://www.thecollegefix.com/umichs-it-department-told-to-stop-using-word-picnic-it-could-harm-morale/

[51] What is a refugee? (United Nations High Commission for Refugees). https://www.unhcr.org/what-is-a-refugee.html

[52] Naturalizations, (Department of Homeland Security), https://www.dhs.gov/immigration-statistics/naturalizations

[53] Cindy Carcamo, Immigration fact check: "Who built the cages?" (Los Angeles Times, Oct 27, 2020).

[54] Department of Homeland Security, FY 2016 ICE Immigration Removals (DHS, 2016), https://www.ice.gov/removal-statistics/2016

[55] Department of Homeland Security, https://www.ice.gov/features/ERO-2019

[56] Nardine Saad, Journalist Bari Weiss skewers New York Times in her resignation letter, (The Los Angeles Times, July 2020), https://www.latimes.com/entertainment-arts/story/2020-07-14/bari-weiss-new-york-times-resignation

[57] Historical Survey, Slave-Owning Societies (Encyclopedia Britannica). Retrieved from https://www.britannica.com/topic/slavery-sociology/Historical-survey

[58] The original data base, released in 1999, was researched and assembled by Emory University historian David Eltis, University of Hull (England) Professor David Richardson, and Victoria University (Wellington, NZ) instructor Stephen Behrendt. The current downloadable file records details of 36,110 slave ship voyages. https://www.neh.gov/humanities/2010/septemberoctober/feature/gross-injustice

[59] David Eltis and David Rischardson, editors, The Trans-Atlantic Slave Trade Database, https://www.slavevoyages.org

[60] U.S. Constitution, Article I, §1, para. 3

[61] U.S. Constitution, Article I, §9

[62] U.S. Census Bureau, 1860 census.

[63] U.S. Public Law 9-22 §1, Ninth Congress, 2nd session.

[64] Daniel C. Littlefield, The Varieties of Slave Labor, (National Humanities Center), http://nationalhumanities-center.org/tserve/freedom/1609-1865/essays/slavelabor.htm

[65] Du Bois was also the first black to earn a PhD from Harvard, co-founded the NAACP, and was the most famous advocate for Blacks in the early 20th century.
W.E.B. Du Bois, The Health and Physique of the Negro American (Atlanta University, 1906). Page 110

[66] Rachel Parker Plummer, 21 Months A Captive: Rachel Plummer Parker and the Fort Parker Massacre (Annotated) (Independently published 2016) page 57, Kindle edition.

[67] U.S. Supreme Court case: Dred Scott vs. Sandford

[68] The 11 states that seceded were Alabama, Arkansas, Florida, Georgia, Louisiana, Mississippi, South Carolina, North Carolina, Tennessee, Texas, and Virginia

[69] <u>Civil War Casualties</u>, (American Battlefield Trust). Retrieved from https://www.battlefields.org/learn/articles/civil-war-casualties

[70] Shirer, William L., <u>The Rise and Fall of the Third Reich</u>, (Rosetta Books. Kindle Edition)

[71] W.E.B. Du Bois, <u>The Souls of Black Folk</u> (Transaction Publishers, 1998) page 64

[72] "African Americans and Education During Reconstruction: The Tolson's Chapel Schools" (National Park Service). Retrieved from <u>https://www.nps.gov/articles/african-americans-and-education-during-reconstruction-the-tolson-s-chapel-schools.htm</u>

[73] Timeline - The 1880s. Retrieved from <u>https://americasbesthistory.com/abhtimeline1880.html</u>

[74] W.E.B. Du Bois, <u>The Souls of Black Folk</u> (Transaction Publishers, 1998) page 49

[75] W.E.B. Du Bois, <u>The Souls of Black Folk</u> (Transaction Publishers, 1998) page 22

[76] Richard Rothstein, "The Color of Law: A Forgotten History of How Our Government Segregated America (Liveright. Kindle Edition), location 500

[77] Gavin Wright, <u>The New Deal and the Modernization of the South</u> (ResearchGate) page 20.

[78] GovTrack.us,
1964 Civil Rights Act, House: https://www.govtrack.us/congress/votes/88-1964/h182

1964 Civil Rights Act, Senate: https://www.govtrack.us/congress/votes/88-1964/s409

1965 Voting Rights Act, House: https://www.govtrack.us/congress/votes/89-1965/h87

1965 Voting Rights Act, Senate: https://www.govtrack.us/congress/votes/89-1965/s78

1968 Fair Housing Act, House: https://www.govtrack.us/congress/votes/90-1967/h113

1968 Fair Housing Act, Senate: https://www.govtrack.us/congress/votes/90-1968/s346

[79] W.E.B. Du Bois, The Souls of Black Folk (Transaction Publishers, 1998) page 3

[80] Lecrae, 7:40: https://www.nydailynews.com/news/national/ny-chickfila-shoeshine-20200623-dasxpjt7arhjlecsrbwou2myrq-story.html

[81] https://www.cnn.com/2020/06/01/business/black-ceos-george-floyd/index.html

[82] The 116th Congress (2019-2021) has 2 black Senators (2%) and 56 Representatives (13%). Black mayors serve 10 cities with populations of 100,000 or more.

[83] http://www.citymayors.com/mayors/black-american-mayors.html

[84] Chicago Police Department, Crime Statistics, (Chicago Police Department, 2020, November 8) https://home.chicagopolice.org/statistics-data/crime-statistics/

[85] FBI Uniform Crime Reporting Program

[86] Diedre McCloskey, Slavery Did Not Make America (Reason, 2018), https://reason.com/2018/07/19/slavery-did-not-make-america-r/

[87] Isaac Ehrlich, Adam Cook, Yong Yin, <u>What Accounts for the US Ascendancy to Economic Superpower by the Early Twentieth Century? The Morrill Act-Human Capital Hypothesis</u> (State University of New York at Buffalo), https://www.journals.uchicago.edu/doi/abs/10.1086/697512

[88] U.S. Census, (U.S. Census Bureau 2019), Wyoming

[89] Du Bois, Harvard University's first PhD, was a black sociologist, activist, and author

[90] History.com Editors, <u>Chinese Miners Are Massacred In Wyoming Territory</u> (A&E Television Networks, 2020): http://www.laweekly.com/how-los-angeles-covered-up-the-massacre-of-17-chinese/

[91] https://www.history.com/this-day-in-history/whites-massacre-chinese-in-wyoming-territory

[92] Erin Blakemore, <u>The Grisly Story of America's Largest Lynching</u>, https://www.history.com/news/the-grisly-story-of-americas-largest-lynching

[93] U.S. Census, 2019: 18.4% Hispanics, 12.8% Blacks alone

[94] Nicholas D. Dauphine, <u>Hispanics – The Forgotten Class in Civil Rights History</u>, (President Lyndon B. Johnson Library): http://www.lbjlibrary.org/education/civil-rights-today-essay-contest/hispanics-the-forgotten-class-in-civil-rights-history

[95] Arthur Schaper, <u>Reparations for Slavery: Be Careful What You Wish For</u> (Town Hall, 2019): https://townhall.com/columnists/arthurschaper/2019/04/08/regarding-reparations-for-slavery-be-careful-what-wish-for-n2544398

[96] Thomas J. Pressly, <u>The Known World of free Black Slaveholders: A Research Note On the Scholarship of Carter G. Woodson</u> (University of Chicago Press, 2006), pp 81-87

[97] Agriculture of the United States In 1860 (Government Printing Office, Washington, D.C. 1864)

[98] W.E.B. Du Bois, The Souls of Black Folk (Transaction Publishers, 1998) Page 45-46, 48

[99] Henry L. Gates, Jr., The Truth Behind '40 Acres and a Mule', https://www.pbs.org/wnet/african-americans-many-rivers-to-cross/history/the-truth-behind-40-acres-and-a-mule/

[100] GEN. Howard's Report: http://civilwartalk.com/threads/the-cost-of-the-freedmens-bureau-1868.150947/

[101] Mike Konczal, No, we don't spend $1T on welfare each year, (The Washington Post, 2014): https://www.washingtonpost.com/news/wonk/wp/2014/01/12/no-we-dont-spend-1-trillion-on-welfare-each-year/

[102] Ivan Pereira, Asheville city council approves reparations plan as Providence explores idea (abc News, July 2020): https://abcnews.go.com/US/city-council-asheville-north-carolina-unanimously-approves-reparation/story?id=71795059

[103] How Fast Is Knowledge Doubling? (Lodestar Solutions), https://lodestarsolutions.com/keeping-up-with-the-surge-of-information-and-human-knowledge/

[104] W.E.B. Du Bois, The Souls of Black Folk (Transaction Publishers, 1998) page 49

[105] Of the five players who led the league in fouls for three seasons, Shawn Kemp, DeMarcus Cousins, and Darryl Dawkins were Black; Vern Mikkelsen and George Mikan were White.

The most personal career fouls were assessed on Kareem Abdul Jabbar, Karl Malone, and Robert Parish . Retrieved from https://www.basketball-reference.com/players/m/mikkeve01.html

R.J. Ross

[106] Raymond Brescia, <u>Wells Fargo Settlement: An important victory for minority homeowners, communities</u> (PBS, 2012), https://www.pbs.org/wnet/need-to-know/opinion/wells-fargo-settlement-an-important-victory-for-minority-homeowners-communities/14150/

[107] Peggy G. Carr, PhD., <u>A First Look at the 2015 Program for International Student Assessment Financial Literacy Results</u> (U.S> Department of Education, May 24, 2017). Retrieved from https://www.treasury.gov/resource-center/financial-education/Documents/NCES%20U.S.%20PISA%20Results%20for%20Financial%20Literacy%20Presentation.pdf

[108] Black Demographics, (from U.S. Census data), https://black-demographics.com/households/african-american-income/

[109] Rachel Hinton, <u>Another billionaire weighs in on state's attorney's race: George Soros gives $2m to group backing Foxx</u> (Chicago Sun Times, Feb 20, 2020). Retrieved from https://chicago.suntimes.com/politics/2020/2/20/21146269/george-soros-kim-foxx-bill-conway-states-attorney

[110] Staff, <u>How George Soros rewarded his St. Louis asset Kim Gardner</u> (World Tribune, August 6, 2020). Retrieved from https://www.worldtribune.com/how-george-soros-rewarded-his-st-louis-asset-kim-gardner/

[111] Lia Eustachewich, <u>California DA's new policy to consider looters' 'needs' before charging them</u> (The New York Post, September 2, 2020). Retrieved from https://nypost.com/2020/09/02/das-policy-to-consider-looters-needs-before-charging-them/

[112] Andrew Ackerman, <u>Fed Moves To Overhaul Lending Rules for Poorer</u> Communities, (The Wall Street Journal, Sep 2020); https://www.wsj.com/articles/fed-to-propose-overhaul-of-lending-rules-for-poorer-communities-11600695600?mod=djem10point

[113] 2019 SAT Suite Annual Report, (College Board, SAT Suite Annual Report, Total Group. ERW: Evidence-based Reading and Writing. 11th Grade Benchmarks: ERW: 480; Math: 530 https://reports.collegeboard.org/pdf/2019-total-group-sat-suite-assessments-annual-report.pdf

[114] California University President Janet Napolitano, Action Item, College Entrance Exam Use In University of California Undergraduate Admissions (Office of the President, University of California, May 21, 2020). Retrieved from https://regents.universityofcalifornia.edu/regmeet/may20/b4.pdf

[115] Admissions Office, Freshman admit data (University of California, as of June 2020). Retrieved from https://admission.universityofcalifornia.edu/campuses-majors/freshman-admit-data.html

[116] Income and Poverty in the United States: 2018, (United States Census Bureau), https://www.census.gov/library/publications/2019/demo/p60-266.html

[117] Historical Poverty Tables, (The U.S. Census Bureau), https://www.census.gov/data/tables/time-series/demo/income-poverty/historical-poverty-people.html

[118] Neil Bhutta, Andrew C. Chang, Lisa J. Dettling, Joanne W. Hsu, Disparities in Wealth by Race and Ethnicity in the 2019 Survey of Consumer Finances (Washington Board of Governors of the Federal Reserve System, September 28, 2020), https://www.federalreserve.gov/econres/notes/feds-notes/disparities-in-wealth-by-race-and-ethnicity-in-the-2019-survey-of-consumer-finances-20200928.htm

[119] Darrick Hamilton and William Darity Jr., Can 'Baby Bonds' Eliminate the Racial Wealth Gap in Putative Post-Racial America? (The Review of Black Political Economy, 2010) 37:2017-216, page 213

[120] Uniform Crime Reporting Program (Federal Bureau of Investigation, 2017)

[121] Robert Woodson, Why Anti-Poverty Programs Often Fail. Retrieved from https://www.youtube.com/watch?v=I2CfiqBa9m8&feature=share&fbclid=IwAR3yeacXSKdisvZxES-eUC0lbR05vxaJbEMBqaF0z-QlUyJvYCDUFZPDQsU

[122] Fatal Force, (The Washington Post), https://www.washingtonpost.com/graphics/investigations/police-shootings-database/

[123] The percent of Whites in each threat category who were killed by police is the same within 1-2%.

[124] From Law Enforcement Officers Feloniously killed (Federal Bureau of Investigation, 2017), Table 42 and U.S. Census Bureau. Retrieved from https://ucr.fbi.gov/leoka/2019/topic-pages/tables/table-42.xls and https://www.census.gov/quickfacts/fact/table/US/PST045219

[125] Centers for Disease Control and Prevention Fatal Injury Reports, National, Regional and State, 1981 – 2018. Retrieved from https://webappa.cdc.gov/sasweb/ncipc/mortrate.html

[126] Will Witt, Are the Police Targeting Unarmed Blacks? Retrieved from https://www.youtube.com/watch?v=GYUQ8_Sf6Kc

[127] United States Department of Justice, Civil Rights Division, Investigation of the Ferguson Police Department (Washington, D.C.: Government Printing Office, 2015), p. 2

[128] Marc Caputo, Weed, fights and guns: Trayvon Martin's text messages released, (The Miami Herald, July 9, 2013), https://www.miamiherald.com/news/state/florida/trayvon-martin/article1951821.html

[129] United States Department of Justice, Department of Justice Report Regarding the Criminal Investigation Into the Shooting Death

of Michael Brown by Ferguson, Missouri Police Officer Darren Wilson (U.S. Government Printing Office, Washington, D.C., March 2015), p. 86.

[130] Glenn Kessler, "Harris, Warren ignore DOJ report to claim Michael Brown was 'murdered'", The Washington Post, Aug 13, 2019

[131] From Expanded Homicide Data (Federal Bureau of Investigation, 2017), Table 6. Retrieved from https://ucr.fbi.gov/crime-in-the-u.s/2018/crime-in-the-u.s.-2018/topic-pages/tables/expanded-homicide-data-table-6.xls

[132] Statement of Charges (District Court of Maryland for Baltimore County, April 12, 2015), https://kniferights.org/263171878-Freddie-Gray-Charging-Documents.pdf

[133] U.S. Department of Justice 2017; https://www.justice.gov/opa/pr/federal-officials-close-investigation-death-alton-sterling

[134] USA Today, https://www.usatoday.com/story/news/nation/2020/08/25/breonna-taylor-louisville-police-search-home-report/3438887001/

[135] State of MN Statement of Probable Cause 27-CR-20-12646, 5/29/2020

[136] KARE News, https://www.kare11.com/article/news/local/george-floyd/new-court-docs-say-george-floyd-had-fatal-level-of-fentanyl-in-his-system/89-ed69d09d-a9ec-481c-90fe-7acd4ead3d04

[137] https://www.ajc.com/news/crime/early-results-show-fulton-da-challenger-in-the-lead/X23G6PDMIFBVHJKYH6UVTQMQ54/

[138] The U.S. Sun, https://www.the-sun.com/news/997939/rayshard-brooks-probation-prison-dui-arrest-wendys/

[139] Cambridge Police Department Incident Report #9005127, 7/16/2009

[140] Bureau of Justice Statistics, Summary, NCJ251145, Oct 2018. https://www.bjs.gov/content/pub/pdf/cpp15_sum.pdf

[141] Fatal Force, (The Washington Post, as of Dec 5, 2020) https://www.washingtonpost.com/graphics/investigations/police-shootings-database/

[142] Atlanta Police Department Weekly COBRA Report as of 12/05/2020. Retrieved from https://www.atlantapd.org/Home/ShowDocument?id=3619

[143] Becky Pringle, A Message from NEA President Becky Pringle (NEA Policy Playbook, 2020), page 1

[144] Fixing America's Police Recruiting Shortage (National Police Support Fund, June 2016). Retrieved from https://nationalpolicesupportfund.com/fixing-americas-police-recruit-shortage/

[145] https://www.youtube.com/watch?v=GdB8AJiDLlI https://www.youtube.com/watch?v=WNKxXqrKDjY

[146] Tim Wronka, Charter Communications, July 2020. https://www.baynews9.com/fl/tampa/news/2020/07/09/city-of-st--petersburg-announces--reimagining--of-policing

[147] U.S. Department of Justice Press Release Number 15-221, updated August 26, 2015, https://www.justice.gov/opa/pr/federal-officials-close-investigation-death-trayvon-martin

[148] https://www.youtube.com/watch?v=8J68p5l-gjQ

[149] Huffington Post, July, 2017. Retrieved from https://www.huffingtonpost.ca/james-di-fiore/black-lives-matter-toronto-yusra-khogali_b_14635896.html

[150] Thomas Sowell, <u>Discrimination and Disparities</u> (Basic Books, Kindle edition), page 175.

[151] Roudabeh Kishi and Sam Jones, <u>Demonstrations & political Violence in America: New Data for Summer 2020</u> (Armed Conflict Location & Event Data Project (ACLED)). Retrieved Dec 17, 2020 from <u>https://acleddata.com/2020/09/03/demonstrations-political-violence-in-america-new-data-for-summer-2020/</u>

[152] Mychal Massie, <u>What if Africans had stayed in Africa?</u> (The Daily Rant, July 2020). Retrieved from https://mychal-massie.com/what-if-africans-had-stayed-in-africa/

[153] <u>U.S. School Spending Per Pupil Increased for Fifth Consecutive Year, U.S. Census Bureau Reports</u> (United States Census Bureau, May 2019). https://www.census.gov/newsroom/press-releases/2019/school-spending.html

[154] Thomas Sowell, <u>Discrimination and Disparities</u> (Basic Books, March 2019) page 150, Kindle version

[155] Douglas Kierdorf, <u>Getting to know the Know-Nothings</u> (The Boston Globe, Jan 2020). Retrieved from <u>https://www.bostonglobe.com/ideas/2016/01/10/getting-know-know-nothings/yAojakXKkiauKCA-zsf4WAL/story.html?outputType=amp</u>

[156] <u>Nonfarm Sole Proprietorship Statistics</u> (Internal Revenue Service, 2016). Retrieved from <u>https://www.irs.gov/statistics/soi-tax-stats-nonfarm-sole-proprietorship-statistics</u>

[158] Independent dealers sought legal protection from manufacturers opening their own dealerships and abusing their relationship with the independents as they competed against them. Tesla has no independent dealers.

[159] <u>Timeline of events in shooting of Michael Brown in Ferguson</u> (Associated Press, August 8, 2019). Retrieved from <u>https://apnews.com/article/9aa32033692547699a3b61da8fd1fc62</u>

R.J. Ross

---

[160] Dr. Thomas Sowell, <u>A Legacy of Liberalism</u> (Creators, November 2014), https://www.creators.com/read/thomas-sowell/11/14/a-legacy-of-liberalism

Made in the USA
Columbia, SC
21 January 2021